In the Heart of a Child

A Journey of Healing and Self-Discovery

Nyssa Wilder

In the Heart of a Child

Copyright © 2014 by Nyssa Wilder

All rights reserved, including the reproduction in whole or in part in any form.

ISBN: 069228625X
ISBN 13: 9780692286258
Library of Congress Control Number: 2014916014
Nyssa Wilder, Cary, NC

I dedicate this book to all of my angels
Thanks for sharing my journey
With sincere love and gratitude

Acknowledgments

I would like to express my deep gratitude to all of the courageous Adult Children of Alcoholics (ACOAs) who have sought their own healing and recovery. The love and support I received within the safe haven of ACOA meeting rooms has been invaluable to me and I know would not be possible without each individual who came before me.

I would also like to thank the founders of the AA and ACOA programs for providing a framework for recovery for adults who grew up with chemically or emotionally addictive parents. The fellowship, education, and support network provide a supportive and collaborative environment that can ease the suffering and loneliness of anyone trying to overcome childhood dysfunction.

Contents

Preface ix

How to Use this Book xi

PART I
Pieces of the Puzzle 1

PART II
The Road to Recovery 55

PART III
A Final Gift 85

PART IV
Recovery Tips 97

PART V
Resources 131

Preface

At some point in my twenties I started telling myself, "I'm going to figure it all out before I'm thirty." Exactly what "It" was I had no idea, but somehow from somewhere this mantra started repeating itself in my head. It's one of several that came to me out of the ether over the years, showing up uninvited, whose purpose seemed to be to point me in a new direction; a direction I had no idea I wanted and desperately needed to go. I eventually came to recognize these mantras as messages from myself. Not my ego-self or physical-self that so many of us tend to relate with, but my true self. The self that I believe existed before that fateful day; the day my soul shattered into a million pieces.

That "fateful day" was my birthday and I imagine I arrived wet, messy, and screaming just like any other newborn being pushed and squeezed into the world. Unlike other newborns, however, I was not exactly greeted with smiles and joy. Actually, based upon what I learned when I was twelve, I'm pretty sure they wished I hadn't shown up at all. In a very short time I went from the warm, comforting surroundings of my mother's womb to a life that would steal my innocence, my trust, and my faith.

What followed was a painful, dark journey that I often did not think I was going to survive. Many times, like Humpty Dumpty, I found myself trying to put all the pieces back together again. What carried me through today, however, is a light that over the years has reflected back to me my true essence and continues to champion me through each step of the recovery process. Who would have thought that learning to love yourself could be so painful? I believe this light to be the source of my mantras as well as the many angels that have shown up to love me, guide me, and help me navigate the storms. My angels are amazing people who somehow knew what I needed to learn, reflected back to me who I really am, and helped me become who I want to be.

I find it amazing how persistent and resilient the spirit is, how it longingly calls me out of the abyss, despite the barriers of hurt, sadness, and loneliness I mount against its presence.

This book is my effort to honor this light and reflect it back to the universe. It is the story of my journey to wholeness supported by God's love and the many angels who lifted me on their wings until I could find my own. I have read many books throughout the years that helped me understand what happened to me as a child and without them I know I would be lost. I hope this book finds those who need it. You are not alone.

How to Use this Book

This book is written in five sections. The first three sections describe my journey; the story of my experience growing up with two alcoholic parents and my subsequent recovery through the grace of God and the use of the Adult Children of Alcoholics (ACOA) program and network. If the term God poses a challenge for you I offer you the wisdom of the ACOA program and suggest inserting the word love, universe, higher power or any other term that aligns with your belief system. ACOA is not a religious program, despite the fact that it uses the Twelve Steps of Alcoholics as a vehicle for recovery. I have come to believe we are all part of the Divine One, regardless of our religious backgrounds and beliefs. I only use the term God because it was my experience and my frame of reference.

The fourth section outlines my personal recovery tips; principles I learned along the way that made the healing possible for me. These are specific to my experience and may or may not work for you. Another bit of ACOA wisdom: take what you want and leave the rest. If you are open, I believe the message you need to hear will present itself. I do not believe it is a coincidence that you are reading this book.

The fifth section is a short resource guide which highlights relevant books, fellowships, organizations, and websites. These resources have provided me tremendous support throughout the years, offering multiple paths and perspectives on healing. Often when I was not open to receiving from one source, the message I needed to hear came to me through a different vehicle. The universe is pretty amazing—love always finds a way.

I recommend reading the entire book through first. This will give you my perspective and a better understanding of the recovery tips. After that, I recommend using it as a support resource during those challenging times, which will no doubt occur if you relate to my story. The recovery tips can be re-read collectively or individually as needed and the resource guide can provide additional information as you embrace your own growth and healing.

My thoughts and prayers are with every person who has to overcome the negative effects of living with an alcoholic parent. I know from personal experience that the road to recovery is not easy and it can sometimes feel extremely long and lonely. I have learned, however, that the healing is definitely worth it. I wish you love and peace on your journey to wholeness.

Namaste,

Nyssa

Part I

Pieces of the Puzzle

A Bridge Appears

In 1995, at the age of 28, I ended the first significant romantic relationship of my life. The relationship lasted almost eight years and although I was the one who decided to leave, when it was over I was devastated. In the process of grieving the loss of my boyfriend, I also grieved the loss of his entire family; a family that was more valuable to me then they knew. Sadly, I did not possess the coping skills to function after that. It took me almost a year to pull myself out of the dense fog that plagued my days, but the grief, tears and lethargy lingered. As time passed, instead of healing, my spirit grew heavier. The weight became increasingly unbearable and my will to face another day slowly slipped from my grasp.

On one of my darkest days, when the emotional pain was piercing my heart, I started having suicidal thoughts. Although suicidal thoughts were not new to me, it had been a very long time since I experienced this cavernous black hole and the darkness was swallowing me. I remember being in my apartment, wandering from room to room, unable to console myself. I could barely breathe. I crawled into bed and created a cocoon in the blankets hoping for some shelter from the storm, but all I ended up doing was sobbing uncontrollably. Nothing was helping and the pain was escalating. I felt hopeless and completely alone.

Thankfully, by what can only be considered divine intervention, instead of doing any harm to myself I found myself turning the pages of the phone book looking under the Cs, for counselor. I had never seen a counselor before and the idea and the courage to pick up the phone did not seem to be my own. With shaking hands, I dialed the number of a random counselor who was located nearby in my community. When the receptionist picked up, I bluntly told her I needed to talk to someone. Upon reflection, I must have sounded very rude. She asked me if I was an existing patient and I told her no. She went on to explain I would need to schedule a new patient consult and said the first available day was in about three weeks. At this point I was in tears, crying into the phone. My next words shocked me and with a quivering voice I heard myself say, "I need to see someone today; I may not be here tomorrow."

I'm not sure what thoughts ran through the receptionist's head, but she must have been trained well. She did not gasp, condemn, or give any verbal indication that my comment was unusual. Her voice was calm; I could have easily just made a comment about the weather. She simply said, "Can you hold, please?" In what seemed like the longest few minutes of my life, I waited for her to return. When she came back on the line she said, "The doctor can see you at five this evening.

Will that work?" I paused and looked up at the clock; it was just past two thirty. I said, "Yes." As I hung up the phone I breathed a sigh of relief, but I was more terrified than I have ever been in my life.

At five o'clock that evening, out of the dark gloomy clouds, a bridge appeared. The first of many that directed me from the shadows into the light. Anne helped me find that first ray of light as my new counselor and one of the many angels who showed up in my life. I cried through most of that first hour long session, sharing what I could through sobs and incomprehensible sentences. I had no idea what I said or why I was there. With one desperate phone call, my journey to wholeness and self-love began. Although I didn't know it at the time, that one single act of courage would change my life forever.

Removing the Veil

Over the next few months Anne helped me discover the source of my pain. Anne was a perfect fit for me as a counselor and I considered myself lucky to have found such a good match. Considering this was a first attempt at reaching out, the odds of finding a workable, personal connection were not in my favor. Anne was easy to talk with and over time, as I became more comfortable, I was able to peel back the layers of my heart and share with her my more vulnerable core. As it turned out, my inner pain had very little to do with my boyfriend and everything to do with my childhood experiences. Although I knew both of my parents were alcoholics, I was in deep denial with no understanding of how their behavior had affected me. The abuse occurred in the shadows and I did everything I could to keep it there. My memories of the first decade of my life are somewhat sketchy and honestly I'm grateful for that.

In the Heart of a Child

During the early years, leading up to my parents' separation when I was six, the environment in our house was beyond hostile. With my parents drinking and fighting, it often felt like a war zone. There are multiple memories here, but I have discovered they are only fragments suspended in time; missing pieces of a puzzle. I cannot recall one good memory with my parents during these years and have often wondered if happy moments existed. If they did, they are likely lost among the wreckage locked away to protect my fragile mind. What I do remember is sadness and fear, lots of fear. I remember fear for my mother and fear of my mother. I remember dishes being smashed, bottles being thrown, and pets being threatened. I remember being punished and humiliated for everything I did and didn't do. There was no peace and I often cried myself to sleep.

As I grew older, although my parents eventually split, new and different wars were waged and the situation became increasingly worse. My soul died a little more each day. Consequently, I erected walls and engaged in negative behavior patterns that kept me on the outer edge of life. I was present, but unable to fully embrace the love and happiness that should have been my natural inheritance. Although there was some much needed peacetime during my teenage years, it was not enough to repair the damage. Ultimately, battle-scarred and broken, I left home and entered my young adult life unaware of how the trauma negatively shaped my character and personality.

In addition to the insidious abuse that occurs in an alcoholic home, Anne also helped me uncover the years of sexual abuse; the abuse that walks in the open door of an unprotected and unloved child. In one breakthrough session Anne said to me, "At some point you have to accept you were a victim of abuse; this is the only way you can begin to heal." Her words sent shock waves through my body. Never before had I considered myself a victim, much less a victim of abuse. After that particular session, I drove home, walked in the front door and collapsed on the kitchen floor. I spent the entire night there, sobbing and feeling for the first time the soul wrenching pain of what had happened to me. Until then, I had no real awareness of the childhood I missed and the abuse I endured. I buried the pain for so long and now it was surging through my body like a firestorm. At some point, I eventually passed out.

As the months passed, I slowly started to feel better. Anne gave me a number of books to read and the more I learned about the effects of parental addiction on children, the stronger I became. It made me feel less alone, less broken. Because of my quick progress I was able to reduce my meetings with Anne from twice a week to once a week. Anne guided me through my denial and mental blocks while helping me accept that what happened to me was not normal, nor was it my fault. I was a victim, yes, but powerless no. This revelation, more than anything else, helped me to want to heal.

I saw Anne for about nine months. At the nine month mark, almost like a re-birth, she told me I was ready to move on; that I no longer needed one-on-one counseling. Among the many accolades about my strength and courage, she said I had a resilient spirit and had a solid grasp on the reality of the situation. I remember her comments buoyed my spirit. The sincere encouragement from a trusted authority figure in my life was rare and I latched on to her every word. In place of one-on-one counseling, she recommended I attend Adult Children of Alcoholics (ACOA) meetings. She gave me some basic information about the ACOA recovery program and directed me to a local meeting. I was afraid to leave Anne, her being my only connection to my newly discovered and not so normal past, but she assured me I would be all right. She also kept the door open and said I could always return if I needed her. Both her compassion and her extension of continued support bolstered my courage as I embraced my new journey. As I left her office for the last time, I gave her a big hug. I was anxious and fearful, but for the first time hope walked by my side.

The God Factor

As it turned out, I had no real comprehension of the challenging journey ahead of me. Being apprehensive as I was, I did a little research to prepare myself for my first ACOA meeting. Knowing I would be meeting a group of strangers, I felt it would be helpful for me to at least understand how the program worked. I was amazed at how much information was available on the internet and I was initially very encouraged. The goal of the program is to help adult children overcome the negative behavior and thought patterns that result from living with a chemically or emotionally addictive parent. As I knew from personal experience and as validated by the information I gathered, the consequences of living in such an environment result in the potential for numerous challenges. For me some of these included perfectionism, approval seeking, fear of criticism, inappropriate sexual boundaries, an inability to recognize my own accomplishments and feelings of isolation, loneliness, and hopelessness. The information I found purported a safe, supportive, and confidential environment. Based upon my counseling sessions with Anne and the fear of exposure that comes with being a victim this seemed to be the perfect program for me.

Unfortunately, with further research my encouragement turned to dismay and then despair. The one barrier that I was not counting on showed up in spades, and as I dug deeper into the program details I realized God was everywhere. Trust God, Allow God, Admit to God, Let Go and Let God! The more I read all I could think was "Oh, God"! What am I going to do? This was a major block for me. I had given up on God long ago and I certainly did not want anything to do with him now. I felt hopeless and alone all over again.

My anger with and denial of God developed over most of my childhood and lasted well into my adult life until I finally began recovery work in 1998. Both of my parents were Catholic, but abandoned their faith well before I was born. Consequently, the only higher power I was familiar with at a young age was my parents and they did not treat me very well. My father was frequently absent due to his military career and when he was home he was passive and emotionally distant with me. In addition, he regularly made it clear to me that I was not his favorite. I cannot recall the number of times I heard him say, "You know your sister is my favorite, right?" I was never sure how to respond so I would look down, turn, and walk away. In the next moment, when my mother would say, "I love the boys best," my soul would silently cry out; a cry I learned to quiet in so many unhealthy ways. I'm not sure anyone realized or cared that I fell through the gap.

It broke my heart every time and I never understood why I wasn't enough.

Although my father could be distant and verbally abusive my mother was determined to break my spirit. On one occasion, when I was about three years old, I wanted to pour my own cereal at breakfast. My mother of course didn't want to be inconvenienced with what would likely result in a spill, but in my three-year-old way I insisted. In addition my father chimed in and said, "Let her try." As my mother expected, I poured much more cereal than I could eat. Instead of helping me out by pouring some of the cereal back in the box, she poured milk over the overflowing bowl of cereal and hatefully promised me that I would eat every last bit of it. Of course, I could not finish it. To punish me she proudly stored the soggy bowl of cereal on the top shelf of the refrigerator for all to see and tried to force me to eat the leftover cereal for multiple meals in a row. She said I would not get another meal until I finished what I wasted. As I sat at the table later that day and the next morning staring down into what was now an unrecognizable bowl of mush, sadness overcame me. As everyone else was eating freshly prepared food I wondered what to do. My bottom lip quivered and tears spilled down my cheeks. Each time the bowl was placed in front of me I refused to eat. This went on for two days until my father finally intervened and rescued me. As I was dismissed from the table, I looked back to see my mother and father arguing. Although I felt comforted by my father's support, I was not confident that it was a good thing.

On another occasion when I was about five, I remember being severely punished for being afraid. My mother was having a party and as usual sent us to bed so we would be out of the way. Being the youngest, always in the rear, I was the last one up the stairs. As we were climbing the stairs, something fell with a large bang and startled me. Frightened, I screamed and ran up the stairs to my brothers' bedroom. I later learned my mother had stacked a bunch of bags and other miscellaneous items behind the front door which fell over as the five of us climbed the staircase. My brothers laughed at me and it didn't take very long for my mother to storm up the stairs and punish me for disrupting her party. The punishment was excessive and certainly didn't fit the crime. The ridicule I experienced from my brothers as well as the punishment from my mother was overwhelming. There was no concern for my fear and absolutely no comfort for the scared child inside of me.

With my father's absences, I was left to the mercy of my mother and for reasons unknown to me at the time, whether sober or drunk, I was her regular target. When she was sober her treatment of me was less harsh, less mean, but I learned at a very early age it was in my best interest to be invisible while she was drinking. If not, I knew I would suffer her wrath. My constant companions during the time I lived with my mother were criticism, hostility, ridicule, and shame. Consequently, the dominant feeling I lived with was fear and the dominant experience I had was one of isolation. Because of this empty existence, love was just a word I heard other people say. I did not understand its meaning and never experienced its cradling arms.

Friendships are particularly difficult for children who live with chemically or emotionally addictive parents, and my experience was no different. My parents' behavior, especially my mother's, prevented me from having friends while I was young. Most often the relationship would start out seemingly normal, but one chance encounter with my mother while she was drunk or in a depressive, foul mood prevented the potential friendship from blossoming into a fulfilling relationship. Often those children just disappeared. Of course there were also the friendships that never started because of the appropriately cautious parents who knew something was not quite right in our house. Being the youngest and most dependent of the five children this situation did not bode well for me. Without the love of my mother or any friendships to nurture me, the loneliness was suffocating. Although I had my four siblings, supporting each other was not something we learned. We all lived in our own isolated darkness.

I have read that the early years of a child's life are critical for developing parental bonds and giving a child a sense of security in the world. I believe this is true. In addition, I believe those bonds and that sense of security are critical for establishing a healthy belief in a nurturing and loving omniscient power. Because these building blocks were missing from my life, God and I had a very rough start. I recall receiving rosary beads, holiday cards and Bibles from my grandparents, but they provided me no comfort as a child. My grandparents lived in different states and their love and influence in my life was limited to annual visits and holiday gifts. I'm pretty sure they knew what was going on, but not knowing what to do or not having the skills to deal with it, they strategically limited their visits. They were strangers then and continued to be strangers for my entire life.

When I first remember learning about God, I was about five years old. At the time, we were living in Navy housing in San Diego, California. My parents didn't go to church, but one of our new neighbors reached out to me, my sister, and my brothers. We had recently started playing with their children and I think they felt church would do us some good. Whether or not they were aware of the depth of the insanity that regularly took place in our house I don't know. It would have been hard to miss the screaming and yelling and the mountains of beer cans at the side of the road on garbage pickup day. It was an environment that would have undercut the faith of even the strongest of adults, much less a child. Despite this, for a short time after learning about God I did try to believe.

I know it was not a conscious choice. I just liked going to church. I liked the people and the music and it seemed comforting to think that someone was looking out for me. I recall feeling safe while I was there. Unfortunately, I learned that feeling of safety was limited to one hour every Sunday within the four walls of the Calvary Baptist Church. As soon as I left church I was on my own again and the insanity at home was always waiting to greet me.

This was the beginning and end, at least for a while, of my faith in God. Acting on what I learned in church I regularly prayed. I prayed for protection. I prayed for comfort. I prayed for love. I have to admit there were nights in the darkness I actually believed something would change. Unfortunately, despite all the praying, none of those things ever showed up for me. In the heart of a child this is nothing short of betrayal. I had been betrayed by my parents and now God. Who would ever protect me? Who would ever love me? Because none of my prayers were answered, I became hopeless and eventually began praying for death. Although I did not recognize it as such at the time, it was essentially what I was doing. My constant nighttime prayer became, "Please, God, don't let me wake up in the morning." It was an easier fate for me to accept than experiencing the fear and helplessness all over again. At that point in my life, sleep was my only solace and God was nowhere to be found.

This habitual prayer continued for years and became deeply ingrained in my psyche. The effects extended well into my adult life. In times of deep stress or when facing difficult challenges I would automatically revert to this behavior—a reflection of the powerlessness and hopelessness I experienced as a child.

Love

When I was six years old my parents decided it was time to end their relationship. This of course led to the issue of custody. How they decided to manage this was congruent with the dysfunction with which we lived, so essentially they told us we had to choose. There was no guidance or any real concern, we were just told to come to an agreement ... on our own. I'm not sure how much more cruel this could have been. At the time my brothers were nine, eleven, and thirteen and my sister was eight. Considering our ages and our life circumstances up to this point, we did not have the skills to hold a meeting and come to a peaceful agreement. It was a painful experience. My brothers wanted to stay with my mother, and my sister and I wanted to go live with my dad. In the end, although we never came to a real agreement; a decision was made that we would stay with my mother. This was not because we felt safe with her, or that we thought this was necessarily best for us. It was a decision born out of the insanity we lived and what we learned. And long ago, we learned that it was our job to take care of her.

With everyone being afraid to share the news with my dad, I was elected the spokesperson—pushed out of the bedroom under duress and too young to stand up for myself. While reflecting back on this time, I have no doubt this was the beginning of my path to over-responsibility. I remember standing in the small, dark hallway leading to the staircase. My body was hot, filled with feelings of fear and shame; my dad towering over me. As I stared at my feet, in a very soft, almost imperceptible voice I said, "We want to stay with Mom." The moment of silence seemed like eternity and I feared I was going to pee my pants. Just when I thought I couldn't hold it anymore, he said okay and walked away. Although he seemed unaffected by our decision, I was certain then he would never love me.

The separation made it necessary for my mother and the five of us to move out of Navy housing and we very quickly, almost under the cover of darkness, moved to a three bedroom ranch house on Holden Avenue not far from the military base. This was an extremely difficult transition for us both emotionally and financially. My mother's hatred of my father was palpable and she did her very best to create a rift in our relationship with him. She blamed him for everything and consistently degraded him in front of us. We all knew she was a part of the problem, but dared not say anything. Although my father also contributed to my sadness and pain, I desperately wanted and needed to hold on to him. He was my only thread of security, a lifeline that kept me from complete despair. In addition to the emotional stress, we went from living off my father's full income to only a partial income that provided a pittance of alimony and child support. This of course did not help my mother's drinking, which seemed to further impact our resources. She swore she did not spend money on beer, but there was always a 12-pack in the refrigerator and like clockwork she began drinking at noon every day. When we started having to use food stamps it was hard for her to deny. Although we had enough to survive, more often than not the refrigerator shelves were bare and I often wondered if there would be food tomorrow.

Although the change came with many difficulties, the new situation did offer a couple of unexpected blessings that were not completely lost on me. The first blessing had an immediate and direct impact. My parents no longer lived together and I no longer had to endure their regular fights. After years of trying to muffle the screams and the sounds of objects crashing onto the walls and floors, the silence was a welcome friend. After their emotional outbursts, I never knew what to expect when I dared to leave my bedroom. Many nights I remember holding my bladder until it hurt just to avoid the shared bathroom, located in a small hallway adjoining our bedrooms. On one occasion I went downstairs to find my mother in the kitchen standing in a sea of colored glass. She had taken a broom to my father's bottle collection, which he proudly displayed across the top of the kitchen cabinets. Terrified, I turned and bolted back up the stairs hoping she didn't see me. The anxiety that came as a result of listening to the ongoing fights was terrifying and exhausting and I was glad it was over.

The second blessing I did not intellectually and emotionally grasp until years later, but I felt it to my core when it showed up. I had never experienced anything like it before and I knew something was different. The blessing I'm speaking of is love. Unfortunately, up until this time I did not know what it felt like to be loved. My parents did not love themselves or each other and even if they did love me with some warped sense of parental responsibility, they definitely did not show it. Thankfully the universe decided I was due, and love with a capital "L" finally arrived. Although it took me many years to be able to truly trust love, I have no doubt now this was my first encounter.

Raphael was his name and he was a middle-aged, gray-haired, airplane mechanic who befriended my mother at a local bar. Although he came along with my mother's drinking buddies, he was not an alcoholic and I recognized quickly that he was very different. He was genuinely kind. What I remember most about Raphael was his calm, quiet presence and his big smile. He was the first positive male role model in my life and he treated me like I was his own daughter. He was also one of the very few men in my childhood who did not inappropriately touch me. I'm not sure exactly why, but we bonded and he became a constant in my life. He showed the same love and compassion toward my sister and brothers, but they never developed the kind of relationship Raphael and I shared. He became my safe haven; my own special savior and friend.

As I got to know Raphael, I learned he was a widowed father who lost his wife to lung cancer at a very early age. As a result, he was raising his three children alone and like my mother was starting over again. In the beginning it was clear to me that Raphael was interested in my mother, but Cupid's arrow did not make its mark. Despite this, he sincerely cared about my mother and he spent a lot of time at our house trying to help out. When there was no food in the fridge or when my mother was low on cash he never had a problem offering support. Often he would leave fresh garden vegetables and unused airport dinners on our front porch to ensure we had enough to eat. As an airplane mechanic he had access to the leftover flight meals at the end of each day and he would bring the food to us instead of throwing it away. Although we joked about it as kids, if it was not for that food we would have often gone hungry.

Raphael did all the things I imagined a father should do and showed me a level of care and compassion that was foreign to me. He took me to lunch, walks on the beach, tours of his vegetable gardens and sometimes we would just sit on the back porch and talk about our day. He was always sure to inquire how I was doing. "How's school today?" Then he would genuinely listen as I played back the mundane details of my classroom lessons and the playground antics. He had no problem expressing his pride when I brought home good grades or did well on one of my many school projects. This was a very different response than that of my mother. Typically when I brought home good grades or did something well, my mother would congratulate me, but she always found something wrong. In addition, her congratulatory comments usually ended with a snide cliché. The one I recall hearing most was, "Don't get too big for your britches."

Although I did not fully understand her motives at the time, I comprehended enough to know that I should not be proud of myself; I should not find joy in my accomplishments. She also mocked me in front of my sister and brothers and this left me open to additional taunting and criticism. Even then I understood the teasing was born out of their insecurity, none of them did well in school, but my understanding did not help my need to belong and also be proud of myself. I learned to keep my successes to myself and I would excitedly wait to see Raphael again, knowing he would be happy for me.

When I was ten years old Raphael and I were in a car accident together. Based upon the officer's assessment it was Raphael's fault, but Raphael felt strongly otherwise and ended up taking the case to court. Because I was in the car with him, he thought I should attend the hearing and be his witness. I was beyond thrilled. I felt so valued and trusted. During the session the judge inquired why I was not in school and Raphael described in detail to the judge and the entire courtroom my straight A record and expressed repeatedly, "She is a smart kid." He told the judge he thought I could contribute to his case and that I would likely learn more in the courtroom than in the classroom. The judge looked at me with a big smile that I'll never forget. He told Raphael to proceed. The love and support I felt that day carried me through many years. It built my confidence, my trust in myself and helped me to continue to excel academically.

Eventually I moved off Holden Avenue and had to leave Raphael behind. Throughout the years, I have moved several times and did not do such a great job staying in touch. I lived in Arizona until I was eighteen and later my service in the military took me overseas. Despite the distance between us, Raphael always stayed in touch. He called, sent birthday cards, and beautiful flowers always showed up on Valentine's Day. He was the only person from my childhood to attend my college graduation and he, unlike my father, was there to hold my hand at my mother's memorial service. This connection was extremely important to me, especially when I was going through difficult periods and not necessarily reciprocating. Today, Raphael is still a constant in my life. We now live in the same state and we talk and visit regularly.

Over the years my academic achievements became the cornerstone of my personal growth and strength. I shudder to think who I would be today if Raphael had not been there to support and encourage me. He is an angel that provided the most important foundation a child needs—the foundation of unconditional love. I'm not sure exactly when, but at some point I started referring to him as my stepdad. In a way he gave me a real home; a home in his heart that I would have otherwise not known.

Shame and Self-Loathing

Although Raphael brought the light of love into my life, Holden Avenue came with its own darkness. My mother started drinking more and in my father's absence I became a more frequent target. My mother also showed an increased belligerence towards my sister and brothers during these years. This was likely a result of her increased drinking, as well as the change in family dynamics as we all got older and grew in our awareness. Awareness, more than anything else, is a severe threat to an alcoholic. My mother began taking extreme measures, trying to maintain control, and chaos reigned every day.

To survive, I became an expert at stuffing down my needs and feelings while I erected formidable emotional walls that would have challenged even the stealthiest soldier. I remember the constant feeling of walking on egg shells. I became hypervigilant trying to avoid any action that would draw attention to myself or spark anger. Of course this resulted in a paralysis of sorts and I became unable to live or truly embrace life. I was simply too afraid of making a mistake. Out of fear of being punished and humiliated, I kept my thoughts and opinions to myself and I equated silence with safety. I also became a tightly wound perfectionist.

Although my mother caused a tremendous amount of pain, for many years I held on to the hope that she really did love me and that eventually the insanity would stop. I daydreamed about a normal life, a normal mother/daughter relationship. Every once in a while, between the hangover and the next round of drinking, I would catch a glimpse of my real mother; an unexpected kindness, a touch, a smile, a kind word. Sometimes she would even give me a hug. In those moments my heart skipped a beat and I could see the woman beneath the alcoholic haze. I often wondered who she really was. I so badly wanted her to hold me, to tell me she loved me, and that everything was going to be okay, but it never happened.

Instead, I continued to learn it was not acceptable to express my own thoughts and needs, to make mistakes, or to try new things. I became terrified of authority figures and of any personal criticism. I tried very hard to be good enough, pretty enough, smart enough, and helpful enough. Consequently, I lived in a chronic state of anxiety and depression trying to maintain a façade of normalcy. If anyone really knew who I was, what I lived, I was sure they would cringe.

As I grew in awareness and size I became more assertive and the incidents between me and my mother became more severe. Many of these incidents involved physical violence. In one experience I was perched on a stool in the middle of the living room while my mother repeatedly smacked me in the face and pulled my hair. She did this with the assistance of her boyfriend all because I accidently took the wrong bus home from school. What made this experience even worse was that I was surrounded by a small group of their friends lounging in our living room drinking beer. They did nothing to stop the assault and as I looked each one of them in the eyes, shame and self-loathing seared my soul. There were many other incidents like this and with each additional blow I became emotionally hardened. My tears eventually refused to flow.

When the physical violence quit working my mother defaulted to her fail safe weapon; my love of animals. One day I came home from school and she told me I needed to go out back and get the cat from the tree. When I asked how long he'd been stuck up there she said he wasn't stuck; she claimed to have hung him. As I rushed out the back door grief gripped my chest; I couldn't breathe. I arrived at the base of the tree sobbing. Not seeing him hanging there, I frantically started calling his name, but he was nowhere to be found. Later that night when he finally showed up to be fed I was relieved, but the pain did not subside. Although she had said it many times, this was the first time I really believed my mother hated me.

It was not long after that incident I learned the deep rooted source of her hatred and anger. At the age of twelve while witnessing my mother in a drunken rage, she revealed to me that my dad was not my biological father. The information shook me to my core and as I recovered from the shock, I could see a hint of satisfaction in her eyes. She went on to share that she had an affair while my father was deployed and declared, "He is not your father, he does not love you, don't let him fool you." It was not until many years later an understanding eventually started to formulate in my mind. I was the living, breathing manifestation of her infidelity; a constant reminder of her own shame and self-loathing.

Although I received the harshest treatment, my sister and brothers suffered my mother's wrath as well and as they grew older they became less and less willing to tolerate it. I remember refereeing several fights to protect my mother; often I would take a blow in these situations. On one occasion, despite my best efforts, my mother was knocked to the bathroom floor unable to get up. I was terrified and wanted to call for help, but I had learned to hide our family secret too well. I could not fathom telling someone what happened. As my brothers grew in stature my mother needed to compensate for her lack of physical control, so she began making extreme threats in an attempt to balance the scales.

The most horrifying memory I recall is when my sister and I were marshaled out of bed at 2 a.m. so my mother could set the house on fire. Still partially asleep and in our nightgowns, we were marched to the front lawn and told to stay put to ensure we did not go up in flames with our brothers. As I stood on the lawn looking back at the house, my mother standing in the doorway with the red gasoline can in her hand, I was sure I would never see my brothers again. My mother never actually dispensed the gasoline or set the house on fire, but the constant threat of harm eventually took its toll and caused a much greater tragedy. With no positive male role model and nowhere to turn for help, my brothers started drinking and using drugs. The favored drink was beer and the favored drug marijuana. They actually grew marijuana plants in their bedroom closet. I'm pretty sure they drank more beer and smoked more marijuana than they ate in those days.

When I was eight years old the emotional trauma manifested itself physically and we lost my oldest brother Cory in a car accident. He and his best friend were drinking, drugging and driving, the deadly Ds, and not only did they take their own lives but also the life of an innocent father. I'll never forget when the flowers from that family arrived at the funeral home. I found it hard to believe they did not hate us. With Cory's death the environment in our house became much worse. My mother lost her first son and her grief turned to a boiling rage which scalded the rest of us daily. What was already a difficult situation became increasingly unbearable.

Mother Nature

As if there wasn't enough to deal with, Mother Nature decided to bless me with her gifts at the vulnerable young age of eleven. This was visually apparent in my curves and budding breasts and did not go unnoticed by the many men that frequented our house. I developed early based upon comparison to other girls and with my towering height, which made me look older than I was, brought a level of attention that I did not understand or know how to handle. The positive attention felt good, as I received very little of this except when Raphael was visiting, but even in my adolescent mind I knew this particular kind of attention wasn't appropriate. In addition to the physical changes, other changes were also occurring. My normal emotional flat-line fluctuated daily and I began losing my mental stability. The cycle of highs and lows confused and terrified me. After years of mastering emotional numbness, my protective barriers were starting to crack and I feared I was losing control.

My mother did not teach me about puberty or share her own personal experience. I have no doubt this was partly because of her stifled Catholic upbringing, but I also know she had no interest in making things easy for me. As a result, I lacked an understanding of the menstrual cycle and its effect on a young woman's physical and emotional body. What I learned came from my sister and the very limited sex education classes at school. This of course left me ill-prepared for the changes I was beginning to experience. I did my best to manage the necessities, but the additional stressors weighed heavily on my mind. Learning how to use a tampon, washing bloody sheets and finding the money to ensure I had what I needed embarrassed and frightened me.

It seemed my mother was determined to negate any positive attention I received for my new and changing body. The more positive attention men showed me, the more criticism she doled out. According to her, I was growing too fast, eating too much, and before I knew it she was calling me a slut, a bitch, and a whore. The names assaulted me. They were the names I heard whispered in the hallway and locker room at school, but they were always about the other girls. I had no idea how I had become one of them overnight. During what should have been an exciting time in my life, a celebration of sorts, I felt self-conscious and ashamed and I very quickly began to hate my body.

In addition to the lack of love and support, the derogatory labels my mother gave me set the stage for the next four years; one of the darkest and most lonely times in my life. From the age of eleven through the age of fourteen I was repeatedly molested. Their names and faces are a blur and after the first year I lost count. Etched in my mind are their alcohol laden breaths, their calloused hands, and the shame that burned my skin. Some of the men were my mother's friends, others random visitors who occasionally dropped by for a free beer. Some were members of our community; people I babysat for or was otherwise connected to in our limited social circle.

When I was at home, the abuse occurred in the evening after my mother passed out or went to drink at the local bar. When I was out, it happened anytime, anywhere; the bowling alley, the park, the neighbor's house. I was a target and it seemed I wasn't safe with anyone. It usually started out as a hug or back massage; seemingly innocent touches, but it never took too long for their hands to find their way up my shirt, around my breasts, then between my legs. There were also the times I was awakened to find someone in the act, their fingers fumbling in my panties, and I froze with fear. When it moved beyond the fondling, when flesh was touching flesh, I learned to shut off my mind. My memories are vague, but I clearly recall their words. *Let me move a little closer, it won't hurt, it will feel good, doesn't it feel good?*

The odd and difficult thing about it all was that when it was actually happening there were times it did feel good. I did not receive much physical comfort from my mother. If I ignored the shame, the attention and physical stimulation filled a need in me. I so desperately wanted to be held, comforted, and loved. This created even more confusion in my adolescent mind. The mixed feelings of shame and sexual excitement caused me to withdraw even more, shutting myself off for fear of being found out. I knew I couldn't confide in my mother, she would most definitely have blamed me and I was too ashamed and embarrassed to tell Raphael; the one man who could have probably protected me.

Nyssa Wilder

For years I carried a secret guilt. Why didn't I stop it? I was not physically helpless and despite my fear I felt I should have been able to say no. I felt that it must be my fault. I must have deserved it, I must have wanted it. I was a slut, after all. I never told a soul and I hated myself more every day. At the age of fourteen, as if giving in to fate, I finally had consensual sex for the first time and opened a door that became impossible to close. I did my best to push the shameful memories from my mind and quickly learned of the magical powers of alcohol. I had a great role model in my mother after all and stealing beer from the fridge was pretty easy after she passed out each night. As I grew older and my awareness began to expand, the picture became very clear in my mind. I was not safe and my mother was not my ally. I needed to find a way out.

Laughter

Despite the barriers my mother created, my father did try to maintain a relationship with the five of us. Not fully trusting my father's love it was difficult for me to share what was happening at home, but the lifeline remained intact and I was grateful. I didn't learn the truth about our biological connection until six years after my parents' initial separation, and I'm convinced that twist of fate was in my favor. My sister and brothers were significantly affected by my mother's negative influence and I know they, as well as my father, suffered for this. My father wasn't innocent by any means. Many times I witnessed his meanness and adolescent rage and more than once watched him taunt and humiliate my brothers. Still, his attempt to stay in touch impressed and encouraged me. I was always amazed he didn't completely give up. While he was away in the military, he regularly phoned, wrote letters and sent birthday and holiday cards.

Many of these were intercepted by my mother, but when I did receive them I was glad to hear from him and happily wrote back.

After my father retired he settled in Arizona with his girlfriend Louise. In 1975, no longer traveling and with a place to call home he invited me and my sister for our first summer visit. It was the first real vacation I ever had. Getting away from my mother for two weeks provided a reprieve from the insanity and I was finally able to breathe. If only for a short time there was some peace at last. Our visits became a yearly event and over the next four years I developed a relationship with my father that began to nurture me. Although I never really felt that he loved me, I was more and more confident that he at least cared.

During the summer vacations, I also slowly developed a relationship with Louise. In the beginning it was difficult to trust her. It seemed easy to blame her for our family problems, which of course is exactly what my mother did. Each time I returned home, my mother spent an entire week degrading her. Initially I felt guilty for liking her, but soon I realized she was genuinely kind. I sincerely enjoyed the time we spent together. Her positive attitude was contagious and much more powerful than my mother's negativity. I also recognized the affect she had on my father. Although he could still be distant and verbally abusive, he was happy with her and this was clear when we went to visit. The summer visits brought me a completely different experience of life. Living in a home, if only for two weeks of the year, with people who were happy and actually appeared to love each other was new to me. I had to learn to behave differently. I had to open up, learn how to smile. I also had to learn how to engage in a conversation; being asked what I thought or how I felt caught me off guard. Although I was often uncomfortable, at a loss for words, it was much better than my normal depressed state of existence.

My father and Louise always made sure to create memories for us. I know Louise was the driving force, but my father happily went along. She brought out the best in him and while we were there she really helped us see him in a different light. If he was alone, I'm sure we would have been sitting in a bar somewhere, but Louise ensured we experienced a little bit of life. We traveled to different Arizona hotspots; Red Rocks of Sedona, the Petrified Forest, and the Grand Canyon. We also visited a number of different restaurants, museums, and zoos. Louise had a beautiful voice and her singing made the road trips even more enjoyable. What I remember most about these trips was the laughter. Louise had an uncanny perspective of the world, her own personal motto being "Lighten up," and we inevitably ended up rolling in laughter until our lungs and stomach muscles ached for relief. We laughed until we cried and it was wonderfully cathartic. I had never experienced such release.

This was such a stark contrast to living with my mother. At home there was nothing to laugh about, but even if I dared break my silence my mother would surely have thought I was laughing at her. Of course this was something I learned very early not to do. With Louise nothing was too serious and laughter was a given. I remember one plane trip when we flew to her mother's home in Ohio for Christmas. Our laughter got out of control, as it often did, and the flight attendant had to come and tell us to keep it down. Louise wasn't concerned a bit; for a few minutes we laughed even harder. Her spirit completely amazed me and I admired everything about her. It took some time, but with each successive visit my heart opened a little bit more and my smile grew larger. Eventually, I was able to let the laughter in. Louise made it easy and I found I was willing to try. I began to sincerely care for her, my angel of laughter, and our relationship started to fill a hole that I did not yet completely understand.

While the living situation at home continued to deteriorate, my trust in my new relationship with Louise grew stronger. This trust nurtured a confidence in me that eventually allowed me to reach out. I felt that if she was with my father, I could depend on the both of them. After returning home one summer, experiencing an exceptionally violent episode with my mother, I summoned all my strength and courage and called my father for relief. I was terrified, but I told him what happened and gave him an ultimatum. If he didn't get me out, if he didn't do something, I would leave on my own. I don't recall his response or what we said to each other that day, but that act of courage put the wheels in motion. It took some time, but before I was fifteen my sister and I had moved to Arizona and started a new life.

While continuing to get to know Louise she invited me and my sister into her family fold. She had a wonderful extended family that regularly stayed in touch through weekend phone calls and annual family reunions. This was very different from the general malaise that existed in my parents' families. Both of my parents grew up in strict Catholic homes and as adults they generally avoided all family affairs. Calling someone to say hello or see how they were doing was an inconvenience and usually only happened during a crisis or when someone died. Through Louise's family as a model I learned the importance of maintaining family relationships and over the next four years her family became mine. I was amazed at the extension of love and connectedness.

They had their own problems of course, but they loved each other and stayed in touch. In the summertime Louise's niece would come to visit and the two of us developed a fast friendship. I felt more welcome and connected to her family than I ever had with my own.

Although the new living arrangement offered a much happier life for me and my sister, the transition did not come without its challenges. The idea that my mother and brothers were no longer a part of our daily lives caused conflicting feelings, and my sister and I had to learn to function in what was now a more cohesive family unit. We had experienced a significant amount of trauma and although we never spoke about it, the damage was evident in the way we managed even the most basic life skills. Emotional outbursts and long periods of silence and withholding were commonplace. Learning personal boundaries, flexibility, forgiveness, fairness, and trust were not only challenging, but often painful. Learning to be myself and trust that Louise and my father would still want me led to many sleepless nights. I often feared they would abandon me if I expressed my own thoughts and needs. What if they decided I was too difficult? What if they returned me to my mother?

Emotionally it was a long, hard road; a transition that was never fully complete. Although I felt love for them, it was difficult for me to truly believe and trust that they loved me unconditionally. My fragmented relationship with love kept my heart bound with fear and my trust faltered again and again. I was haunted by a question I could never answer. How can anyone possibly love me when my own mother can't?

My sister and I managed the transition to our new life differently and our relationship suffered as a result.

Although I struggled with trust, I wanted and was able to embrace our new home. I sincerely wanted to be happy and Louise made me feel hopeful. My sister on the other hand had more difficulty adjusting and was often angry. We developed a strong survivor bond that carried us through the years on Holden Avenue and after Cory passed away she was my only family connection. When our relationship shifted as a result of the move, it sincerely broke my heart. I didn't know what to do and I didn't understand why she wasn't happy. Her anger threatened me and my new security and I resented her for upsetting our new home. The only thing I knew to do was keep my distance and we slowly grew apart.

As time passed, I accepted the distance between me and my sister and I settled into my new routine. Although I struggled with low self-esteem and depression, I was eventually able to embrace some of the normalcy that came with my new life. I continued to excel in school and I eventually developed my own friendships. With each new success there was growth, confidence, and increased independence. With this new confidence my relationship with Louise became stronger. I began to see her not only as a friend and confidante, but also a mother figure. She took care of everything I needed and never once complained or made me feel I was an inconvenience. She took me out for lunch, clothes shopping, and we even talked about men. She also taught me about fitness. Tennis, biking and walking were part of our routine. But my favorite pastime was the Sunday drive. I had never heard of such a thing and I loved the idea. With the wind blowing in my hair, her beautiful voice filled the air and my heart swelled with love for her. She sincerely treated me like I mattered and each day I believed it more. She did all the things I imagined a mother should do; the things I daydreamed about when I was younger. She gave me what I needed at a very difficult time. Her gift of laughter built a bridge to my heart that ultimately helped me want to live a better life.

My Secret Guilt

There were many good times during the four years I lived in Arizona, but the unresolved issues from my earlier childhood followed me into my new life. I'm not sure how much Louise and my father were aware of, but they never said a word. We didn't talk about the problems and I didn't receive counseling to deal with the fallout of the earlier trauma. I suspect part of the reason for this was that my father was still an alcoholic. Although he now played a more positive role in my life, his disease and subsequent lack of self-awareness prevented him from recognizing my problems and acknowledging the need for professional help. He and Louise were also unaware of the sexual abuse and I did not have the courage to share this information.

As a result of the early childhood trauma and the sexual abuse, I developed a level of promiscuity that served the needy child inside of me; the child that so badly wanted and needed her mother's love. Louise was a wonderful role model in my life, but I was only just beginning to know her affection and the damage had already been done. As I started to date, my low self-esteem and my lack of self-worth came to the surface. My perception of men was severely distorted. On the one hand I was afraid of them and when in their presence I felt self-conscious and ashamed. On the other hand, the power of my sexuality excited me and gave me a sense of being in control. Consequently, I was always on the lookout for male attention and I felt valued if a man found me attractive. I equated my value with the degree of male attention I received and it took me a long time to see things differently.

Mostly, I thought men just wanted sex and this usually happened pretty quickly. On one occasion I brought a friend home from a party and we had sex in the spare bedroom adjacent to the kitchen pantry. I was sixteen years old and my father and Louise were asleep in their bedroom. For the next month I was sick, beside myself with fear and shame. I experienced a haunting guilt. I thought I had lived up to my mother's condemnation; I was truly a slut, a bitch, and a whore. This guilt further fueled the need for attention and validation, and to cope with my destructive behavior I started drinking even more frequently.

The cycle of promiscuity and drinking repeated itself throughout my high school years and continued into my young adult life. For a period of time, alcohol was definitely a problem for me; binge drinking is what I heard it called. I had many close calls, some behind the wheel of a car, and when I look back I'm amazed I survived. I more than once thought that I was subconsciously trying to live out my childhood death wish. I could have easily followed in my brother Cory's footsteps.

Although I did not fully understand it, I developed enough self-awareness to know on some level that my behavior was inappropriate and unhealthy. At the very least, I knew it was not making me happy and I sincerely wanted and needed to change. Whether it was the result of deep emotional pain or the numerous brushes with death, at some point I started referring to the angel on my shoulder. I began to sense deeply that there was a reason I survived not only my early childhood, but also my own destructive behavior.

A sense of purpose began to settle over me. It was on the wings of this angel that my first mantra arrived and although I was still struggling, I repeatedly began telling myself, "I survived for a reason."

Independence

Despite my childhood experience, Louise's support and a little luck carried me through my high school years without any major incidents. As high school passed by I was faced with the challenge of what to do with my future and I embraced the idea of my new independence with excitement. I originally planned to apply to college, a path that filled my father with pride, but I wasn't able to follow through with the necessary commitments. Instead, I enlisted in the US Navy and six days after my 18th birthday I was off to serve my country.

The years in Arizona offered me a much needed reprieve from the years of insanity with my mother, but I had no real understanding of the damage that had been done nor the healing work that was necessary to help me become the person I was intended to be. Because of this I headed out into the world inadequately equipped to cope with everyday life challenges and develop into a fully functioning, healthy adult. After I graduated boot camp and left for the military, Louise and my father split up. Although they never married, their relationship was the most loving adult relationship I had ever experienced and their breakup created a deep sadness in me. The strength and emotional foundation I began building in my high school years started to crumble. The relationship with my fathered deteriorated to the pre-Louise days and I often wondered if Louise still loved me. In my childlike emotional mind, it made sense to me that if she could fall out of love with my father than she could certainly fall out of love with me.

After boot camp I was stationed overseas and the military was fast taking hold of my time and routine. Managing my new experiences with my perceived loss of Louise created a high degree of inner turmoil. My anxiety and depression reared their heads, my self-esteem sunk to a new low, and I felt completely alone in my new world. I was on a ship being tossed about by a hurricane and I did not possess the coping skills to navigate the storm in a healthy way. Because of this I reacted to my world with a strong sense of pride, perfectionism, and superiority; defects in my character I later came to abhor.

Although I initially stayed in touch with Louise, doubt infiltrated my mind and for many years our contact was limited to holiday and birthday phone calls. This was not Louise's fault and I know she wondered why I disconnected. In my defense, I was floundering. I felt abandoned and I was doing my best to cope in the only way I knew how; I stuffed my feelings, put my head down, and kept moving forward. I left the past behind.

In the Heart of a Child

During my military years I was stationed both in the US and overseas. With my travel, I gained a lot of new life experience and had the opportunity to meet many different types of people. I traveled to France, Spain, Italy, Morocco, and a few other small Mediterranean countries. I also lived in England for a year. During these years, I recognized that other people lived very differently than me. They embraced life and didn't appear to struggle with the fear and anxiety that consumed me. As I met new people and observed their behavior, I would often become jealous wanting what they seemed to have, with no idea of how to get it, or even know what it was. I also watched people in my peer group join tours and engage in group activities. I never had the courage to participate. I felt completely inadequate and always feared being judged. What if I said or did the wrong thing? What if I wasn't good enough?

For a long time I felt like an outsider in my own life. Although I still explored and took advantage of some sightseeing and travel, my military experience was significantly diminished due to my fear and insecurity. After five years, I was honorably discharged from the service and this transition, much like my transition to independence, created a significant amount of challenge for me. I was still struggling, responding to my life from a position of fear. Unfortunately, it was still many years before my sense of purpose redirected me.

The Mirror

If it is true that every relationship is a reflection of the relationship you have with yourself, then for many years me and myself were engaged in an unhealthy affair. Not having the healthy role models when I was young, I learned negative behavior patterns that did not serve me well when I tried to engage in romantic relationships. In addition, the sexual abuse left significant emotional scarring that made real intimacy extremely difficult to achieve. Because of this I was attracted to people who were not good for me and I was not aware enough to recognize the pattern. I also did not possess the character traits or interpersonal skills that would have attracted a healthy person. Consequently, for most of my twenties I was treading water. I was struggling to be happy and have a healthy relationship, but I had no concept of what that was or how to achieve it. The attachment issues that developed because of the lack of a mother/

daughter bond made it difficult to fully trust anyone and I continued to find it difficult to believe and actually feel that anyone, much less a man, would really love me.

In my twenties I was involved in two romantic relationships that served as a mirror for me. Each in their own way showed me what I didn't want and who I didn't want be. The first was fairly superficial. We were stationed in England together—two kids away from home for the first time. Our relationship was one of comfort and convenience and for the most part we simply drank and partied our free time away. We never had a serious conversation, and I felt absolutely no connection to him. It was fun, but there was no intention for the future and no real thought about where we were going, what we were doing, or if we should even be doing it together. We were consistently on the go and kept ourselves distracted to avoid looking at the futility of our relationship. I believe the lack of connection is what kept the waters calm, allowing two years to pass by relatively unnoticed.

I knew I wanted out, but unfortunately I did not have the necessary interpersonal skills to navigate this hurdle. I feared confrontation and I had difficulty expressing myself openly and honestly. Because of this, I was unable to proactively end the relationship and sadly it ended painfully, with my infidelity. I was too young to understand the seriousness of my actions and I did not know that there could have been another way. I simply reacted to my need and when I told him he was furious. It didn't help that the exchange occurred over the phone. As he started to cry and shouted a litany of expletives in my ear, I hung up and promised myself I would never let that happen again. It was not my intention to hurt him.

The second relationship lasted about eight years. It was clear from the moment we met there was a connection; a connection I had not yet experienced in my young adult life. His name was Brandon. We worked in the same division and we would often run into each other in the hallways at work. He was half Cherokee Indian and half Irish with a tall, thin and muscular stature made only more beautiful by his dark brown hair and chocolate colored eyes. In addition to his physical beauty, he exuded a level of charisma that left me speechless every time I saw him.

Still very clumsy with my interpersonal skills and having no concept of how to engage in a healthy way, the relationship started with my usual promiscuity. Our first date went well beyond the planned dinner and drinks. Although this was a pattern I was not happy about, we laughed all the way back to the barracks and I remember there was an easy feeling between the two of us. He held my hand and kissed me on my cheek when he said goodbye. When he walked away I was struck by the realization that it was the first time I had ever laughed with a man.

As I drifted off to sleep that night I found comfort in the laughter we shared, but the next day arrived with the same old shame and guilt. I woke up sweating with fear and I hoped I would never see him again. As it turned out, Brandon had other plans. At noon the next day he contacted me at the office and from that day forward we decided we were in a relationship. I did not comprehend how ridiculous our conversation and subsequent decision was; I just knew the comfort and attention felt good.

The first couple of years went by very quickly. We spent time getting to know each other and we were able to travel together before my discharge from the military. We traveled through Italy, France, Spain and Morocco and a few other Mediterranean countries. We frequently went off the beaten path and enjoyed the local fare while meeting new people. Over time I realized we had similar interests and beliefs and it seemed we were a good fit for each other.

When I was with Brandon I experienced a comfort that was new to me. Spending time with him was somehow validating and it allowed me to breathe in my own skin. In the beginning, I sincerely believed our relationship would result in marriage and a family of our own. We were both respected in our personal and professional circles and it seemed we had a great future ahead of us. I fell in love with him and I began to trust his feelings for me. As the relationship became more serious we did the family introductions and I recall we felt happy. I became especially fond of his family. His parents were extremely warm and welcoming and I easily created a bond with them. His mother was a stay at home mom and his dad an electrician. His mother was always there with a smile and an offering of food, while his dad provided a listening ear when I was in need. I recall many nights sitting on the porch visiting with them, finding comfort in their kindness and friendship. They both treated me like a daughter and I loved them for it. When Brandon was discharged from the military we moved to California to be closer to his childhood home and pursue our college degrees.

Despite our connection and some of the wonderful experiences we shared, my relationship with Brandon started to take a turn in the third year. As we grew closer, I began to understand the nature of the bond we shared. It was not a particularly healthy bond, as I learned, but it was a bond that opened a spiritual door for me. Brandon's father was a recovering alcoholic and although he had been sober for over 15 years when I met him, Brandon experienced much of the same dysfunction I experienced as a child. He was spared the sexual abuse, but living with an alcoholic he lived with the same fear, shame, and abandonment for the first five years of his life. Because of this, Brandon and I developed similar character traits as children and engaged in the same negative behavior patterns as adults. Many years later, when reflecting on the night we met, I realized I was not the only one acting out.

Brandon was a perfect mirror for me and I slowly started to understand how unhealthy my behavior was. We both had the same tendencies; stuffing our feelings and long periods of silence were commonplace. Consequently, our communication skills suffered and we were unable to effectively deal with the day-to-day challenges that come with any relationship. We both avoided conflict and we were never able to resolve issues and grow together as a couple. The fear of abandonment terrified us and as a result we stayed stuck, with no way out of the pain. What would typically happen is that one of us would explode. With a drink in one hand, our inhibitions came down, and we would decide it was now time to talk about everything we had previously been too afraid to discuss. At a minimum this resulted in a belligerent argument between the two of us; sometimes it escalated to a fist fight between Brandon and an innocent bystander who came to my aid. Of course, the things we said during these outbursts were often hurtful and the scars began building up on our relationship.

As we struggled through the day to day, we reached a limiting point where we no longer knew what to do. We did not learn the necessary skills growing up and we never realized we should ask for help. It was not even a thought we had. We assumed we possessed all the skills we were supposed to have and we generally rated ourselves as better communicators than most of the people we knew. We did eventually start to talk about our behavior, but unfortunately neither of us was emotionally healthy enough to make a real change. We simply couldn't move past all the unresolved childhood pain. We became steeped in anger and began harboring a lot of resentment. We stuffed all of our adult feelings on top of the old childhood feelings and eventually we were both stuffed full.

Not understanding the seriousness of our situation nor recognizing that need for real help, the damaging behavior continued for the next four years. We continued to ignore the issues and eventually our avoidance took a toll. I buried myself in school work, while Brandon acted out and had an affair. Although he asked for my forgiveness and begged me to stay, the infidelity was too much for us to overcome. I felt abandoned and he felt ashamed. It became increasingly difficult to breathe. I knew it was time to leave and after seven years I eventually had the courage to have that conversation.

I'll never forget the day I moved out. For an hour I lay in his arms and said goodbye. We sobbed like two children saying goodbye to their best friend. We were in so much pain, with no understanding of the real problems and no idea what to do.

Although we were not able to find a way out of the pain together, the experience helped me grow and continue the pursuit of my purpose and a better life. The relationship with Brandon offered a love and connection through both him and his family that presented a mirror whereby I could truly see myself. When I looked in this mirror, I could more clearly see the angel on my shoulder and my mantra, "I survived for a reason," resonated throughout my entire being. My thoughts about my sense of purpose started to dominate my mind and at some point I began telling myself, "I'm going to figure it all out before I'm thirty."

Hopelessness

Embracing my future alone did not come easy. I did not have a good relationship with my mother and father and my communication with Raphael, Louise and my sister was infrequent at best. I left most everything behind to avoid the pain. Ironically, the pain found me anyway. Now I was alone and as I tried to step into my future, my past was holding me back. It took another year for Brandon and I to disconnect completely. Although I was the one who left, I experienced a deep sense of loss and I missed him and his family terribly. He was the first man I ever loved and his family meant the world to me. When he reached out, I couldn't say no. We both had difficulty letting go and we continued to spend time together. We helped each other through the separation both emotionally and financially and we would sometimes comfort each other in the quiet of the night.

Brandon did not want our relationship to end and frequently pleaded with me to reconcile. Our conversations extended into the early morning hours, as we discussed our inability to work through the serious issues that kept us stuck. Each time I thought there was a possibility, the feelings of abandonment washed over me. It was difficult for me to believe we could make another start and in the end my instincts were correct. Almost a year later, in a chance encounter with a friend, I learned Brandon started dating almost immediately after our separation.

As I absorbed this information, grief overcame me and buckled my knees. I could not believe this was happening to me again. More than ever before, I equated my value with his love and I sunk into a deep, deep depression. I felt broken and all alone. I vacillated between outrage and self-pity and the darkness swallowed me. As my spirit tired, I resigned and found myself with an old familiar friend. When I went to sleep each night the hopelessness enveloped me and I prayed, "Please, God, don't let me wake up in the morning."

Part II

The Road to Recovery

The Laundry List

Despite my challenges with God, I did eventually overcome my emotional and spiritual obstacles and begin attending ACOA meetings. As I continued to research aspects of the program, I understood how the program could be helpful, and as it was I had nowhere else to turn. I was still struggling with anxiety and depression and I didn't want to let Anne down. I didn't quite understand that I would also be letting myself down. I had not yet learned that I was worthy of the love and care necessary to heal. I simply told myself I would try the program for a month and worry about the details of my strained relationship with God later.

The first ACOA meeting I attended was in the clubhouse of a townhome community in my neighborhood in northern California. The clubhouse was situated on a large, beautiful lake and the community had an immaculately maintained landscape. Driving in that first night, I noted how peaceful the surroundings were and wondered if the scenery was somehow staged to welcome the nervous newcomer. I was grateful the meeting was nearby. With the emotional and physical energy it required to face my past, I did not have the fortitude to drive a long distance or navigate huge hurdles just to show up. I needed to conserve my energy for the real work, which of course as perceived by me was walking into a meeting full of strangers to reveal some of my deepest darkest secrets.

I got there a little early and waited in my car, contemplating what this new experience might bring. While trying to engage my courage, people passed by and headed toward the entrance. Men, women, young, old, black and white; the diversity surprised me. Still, I sincerely doubted they had the same problems and experienced the same sense of loneliness and hopelessness that consumed my life. I was sure no one was as broken as me. When I got out of the car and started walking toward the entrance, I became paralyzed with fear. My heart began racing, my face and ears became hot, my knees weak, and sweat covered the palms of my hands. I felt seriously ill. Because I took a great amount of pride in being able to handle anything, this fear undermined my confidence and the feelings of vulnerability overcame me.

Vulnerability was not something I learned or could tolerate so I berated myself and quickly talked myself out of the meeting. I decided it was too much to bear, so in defeat I turned to walk away. Thankfully, on that night, the universe had different plans.

Just as I was turning to head back to my car a soft voice called out to me. When I looked back I saw a woman of medium build with short brown hair standing in the doorway waving to me. She looked to be about my age and had the most inviting, disarming smile I had ever seen. No doubt a smile sent specifically for me. Feeling a little ashamed of my fear, I turned around and headed back toward the entrance.

During that first meeting I learned a lot about the ACOA program and, unknown to me at the time, I had met another of my angels. One who would not only guide me for this leg of the journey, but also become a lifelong friend and mentor. Her name was Theresa and as she greeted me at the door, I felt the fear gently release my heart and my pulse slowed to a more normal rhythm. The meeting room had a warm, welcoming environment and it felt very much like a family atmosphere. The members of the group were open and friendly and made me feel comfortable as soon as I walked in the room. Coffee and tea were provided and there was a table covered with books that I later learned I could check out. As I walked around the room meeting the group members, I noted how normal everyone seemed and I anxiously wondered what they saw when they looked at me. Were they judging me? Did they think I was damaged? Could they see in my eyes the shame that bound me?

Soon after I arrived, we were all seated around a large rectangular table staring into our cups of coffee and tea. As everyone looked down at their cups, I looked a little more closely into mine, wondering if it somehow provided a portal to my soul; a portal that would help me better understand how I ended up here. The meeting was very structured. It had a very specific format and there was a designated chairperson as well as a pre-planned theme. On this particular evening, the theme was about surrender and focused around a common ACOA slogan, "Let Go and Let God." When the chairperson spoke, the words rang in my ears and I thought,

Oh God! Here we go again. Not what I needed, as I continued to wipe my palms on my jeans. My internal barriers shot up in defense, my anxiety kicked up a notch and I looked deeper into my cup of tea hoping the portal would somehow help me find a way out.

After the initial comments, several readings were shared out loud and my anxiety started to ease again. The first was How Meetings Work. It was a great explanation of the way an ACOA meeting is conducted and gave me immediate understanding of the way the evening would progress. It also clarified that ACOA is not a religious program and prompted members to replace the word God with Love, Higher Power, Universe or any other term that fit within their belief system. This knowledge provided me a tremendous amount of comfort. In my mind I immediately chose the word Love and I relaxed even more.

In addition to How Meetings Work, there were many other shared readings. Some of these included The Traditions, The Promises, The Twelve Steps and The Solutions. Each was passed around the table and a member could choose to participate and read a few passages if he or she liked. The one that really captured my attention that night was The Laundry List. When I heard the title my mind simply drew a blank. I could not anticipate the possible content or what laundry could possibly have to do with this meeting.

The Laundry List as it turned out had nothing to do with actual laundry; it outlined the common characteristics of adult children of alcoholics. Most of the traits I had heard or read at least once before and each resonated with me in varying degrees. The ones that I related with most were isolation, loneliness, fear of authority figures, an inability to stand up for one's self, an overdeveloped sense of responsibility and of course the one I knew I had certainly mastered, stuffed feelings.

When we finished the readings the floor was open for sharing. A member could choose to share a personal story about the theme or any other program topic that may be weighing on their mind. Not sharing was also an option and on that night I was extremely grateful to know that I was not required to speak. It allowed me to relax and just listen instead of focusing on my anxiety or what I might say. Going around the room, some people shared recent events and some drew from the past. Some talked about their grief, while others talked about their newfound joy. Each person spoke about what happened and how it made them feel. A couple of people, who had clearly been with the program a long time, talked about how they recognized their unhealthy attitudes and behaviors and how they had learned to respond differently with their new ACOA tools.

As I sat there listening and looking around the room at what was a very diverse group of people, it dawned on me that I was sitting in a room with a group of people that were just like me. With each story, my recognition of our shared journey began to settle in my soul. For a moment it was as if I stepped outside of myself; I was only an observer. My heart was beating in my head, my eyes welled with tears. I realized, for the first time in my life, that I was no longer alone. This deep loneliness I carried within me was not unique to me. It was not the result of faulty wiring, weakness, or anything I may have ever done to deserve such despair. Once again I heard Anne's words, "It was not your fault," and they soothed me like never before.

I felt conflicted as empathy, sorrow, and gratitude washed over me. These people, my new friends, had traveled a similar path and each had experienced at least some of what I had as a child. My heart broke for each of them, but I was sincerely grateful they were here with me now. After listening, I knew deep within my being that this was a group of people who would not only suspend judgment, but who would also understand, listen, and simply accept me as I am. It was one of the most comforting, soulful experiences I've had in my lifetime and I felt a spiritual shift occur inside of me. Later, while I was reflecting upon the meeting and processing my feelings, I decided The Laundry List was an appropriate title. After all, it dealt with those areas of my spirit that needed to be cleansed, the pain washed away, so I could heal and fully embrace my life. On that night, I decided that maybe God deserved another chance.

Toxic Shame

Although I was willing to open the door, allowing God back into my life full time did not come easy. It took a tremendous amount of painstaking introspection to rebuild our relationship. Despite my best efforts I broke up with him repeatedly during that first year. Many times I swore I would never be fooled again. Gratefully, for my sake, there was a loving force that brought me to my knees time and time again. It took me a while, but each time I found myself at the altar, I could see more clearly into my past and understood more about my parents' behavior. It didn't necessarily help my grief in the moment, but it helped me to keep moving forward and my soul started to heal.

In my recovery work I learned a lot about toxic shame. In a normal, healthy family, shame is a part of learning right from wrong and developing a moral and ethical compass. In a dysfunctional family, however, shame is used to control the child. In many cases the child becomes the scapegoat for all the parents' problems. As a result, instead of the healthy shaming of poor behaviors the parent shames and humiliates the child's actual being. This causes feelings of worthlessness and hopelessness and as I know too well can result in depression and suicidal thoughts.

Shame was a huge barrier to my personal growth and development when I started my ACOA journey. I felt shameful about everything; my family history, my parents' behavior, my own behavior and the joy and happiness that eluded me. I carried the weight of the world on my shoulders and sincerely believed everything was my fault. I also carried a deep shame about the sexual abuse, my own promiscuous behavior, and the person I had become as a result. "Why didn't I stop it?" was a question I often asked myself. For many years these memories plagued me and I wondered if I was defective. Did I really like being violated? It wasn't until several years into my recovery work that I had an "aha" moment and I finally recognized and understood what happened to me.

Although I was physically capable of stopping the abuse, I was emotionally crippled and although I was endowed with speech, I had no voice. I had learned to be compliant as part of my survival and it was so deeply ingrained in my psyche I did not have the ability to think or speak for myself. I did what I was told and that was it. The shame was a breeding ground for fears and irrational beliefs that paralyzed my spirit and silenced my voice.

I relied heavily on the ACOA tools when I started the program. These included The Twelve Steps, meeting attendance, use of the ACOA slogans and support network, and reading personal growth books. I never officially declared a sponsor, but Theresa became a close friend and confidante and helped me through many personal challenges. I learned a lot about myself in that first year. Because of my childhood experiences I developed a number of unhealthy personality traits and ineffective behaviors that negatively impacted my life. Although my perfectionism, withholding, and isolating actions were my biggest enemies, my personal laundry list was very long and I seemed to add to it daily as I grew in awareness. For a long time, my greatest challenge was being honest with myself. Admitting to myself who I was and who I had become was not acceptable to me was heart breaking. Often this increased awareness is what brought me to my knees. Looking in the mirror each day, feeling more damaged than ever, I grieved for the little girl inside of me and I repeatedly told her it was not her fault. I promised her I would fix it and make the pain go away.

What I came to understand is that my experience growing up with two alcoholics created a very unstable foundation on which to build my life. This foundation did not serve my emotional, spiritual, or intellectual growth or well-being, and I soon learned that I needed to rebuild this foundation to be successful with the ACOA recovery process. It wasn't enough to just attend meetings and talk about the problems. It also wasn't enough to just change my behaviors. Simply trying to work on my perfectionism, be less hard on myself, or trying to be more emotionally available and vulnerable was not going to bring about the change I needed. To make real progress and create long-term change I had to address the root causes and let go of all of the negative feelings, thoughts and behaviors associated with the person I had become. Basically, I had to face my fears and change my entire belief system.

In the ACOA program The Twelve Steps of Alcoholics is adapted for adult children and provides a guide for changing one's belief system. From admitting powerlessness and surrendering to God, to making amends and having a spiritual awakening, the steps seemed straight forward enough. I learned very quickly, however, that putting them into practice was an entirely different thing. I often became frustrated and felt like giving up. Thankfully my will to heal was stronger than my fear. If I could achieve even a fraction of the healing I heard about in my first meeting, the struggle was worth it. I would attend another meeting, hear another story and my hope would be renewed that I too could make this work.

Fears and Irrational Beliefs

The most damaging negative message that I received growing up with my parents was that I was not lovable and therefore I did not matter. Because my thoughts, needs and feelings were shamed, I deeply internalized my lack of importance over the course of my childhood. For most of my early childhood I felt invisible and actually practiced my invisibility to avoid being noticed. I have sometimes thought this is why I can't remember most of it. In my mind I didn't exist. I was merely a shadow.

Of the many fears I've battled and had to extricate, my most dominant fears were fear of abandonment and fear of authority figures. Abandonment, of course, is death to a child and when the threat of abandonment is being wielded like a sword by an adult, trust in authority figures is damaged. Without trust, fear grows. I recognized through my recovery work that living with an alcoholic is like being abandoned daily. I also learned this sense of abandonment can be brought into the present moment through memory, thereby negatively impacting life in the now.

I remember a story my father told me when I was about thirty-five. He recounted a two-year-old temper tantrum I had in the back seat of his car as we were leaving a grocery store parking lot. He said I wouldn't shut up so he stopped the car at a nearby Dumpster, put me in it and walked away for a few minutes. He said when he came back I was finally quiet, but the look on my face was one of pure devastation.

In that moment, before he finished the story, I was two again and the room began to fade. I was not sure what made me more sick—the fact that he did it in the first place or that he was so casually sitting there telling me the story now. As I recovered and looked him in the eye, I reflected on the destructive power of alcoholism. I had been involved in ACOA for a long time at that point and I had a comprehensive understanding of the disease. Even at this advanced point in his life, where one would think age would bring maturity or at least a little wisdom and understanding, he did not grasp the tremendous cruelty of his actions. He did go on to say the look haunted him and he swore to himself that he would never do anything like that again, but I have to imagine he was not true to his word. As I got older I came to believe I was the cause of all the pain in my family, and I was responsible for all of my parents' thoughts, feelings, and behaviors. If I could have rationalized being put in the Dumpster in my two-year-old mind, I'm sure I would have thought it was my fault. I somehow deserved to be thrown away. This of course set my adult-self up to be a caretaker and a people pleaser, which negatively affected my ability to develop as an individual and take care of my own needs.

Other fears that were directly related to my fear of abandonment were fear of criticism and fear of failure. These manifested in my personality as perfectionism and were deeply rooted in my irrational belief that if I could be good enough, smart enough, and pretty enough my parents would have to love me. Of course this wasn't true and as I experienced each successive setback, I became even harder on myself. As an adult I continued to hold myself to extremely high standards, but I was now instead seeking love and validation from others trying to fill the gaping hole my parents left behind.

Letting Go

One of the most difficult aspects of my recovery work was learning to manage the relationships that influenced my life. In order to progress on the path of recovery and ensure my own healing and growth, there were relationships I needed to nurture and others where I needed to let go. The most challenging of these to process were the relationships within my immediate family. This was especially true when it came to my parents. While reflecting on my relationship with my parents, I recognized there were many times in the past when I thought I had already let go. After all the pain and the years of disappointment, I was convinced I didn't need them nor did I care that they were not emotionally available to me. What I learned through recovery, however, is that I was lying to myself. I was engaging in an old pattern of stuffing my feelings and pretending I was okay. The truth of the matter was that there was a child inside of me that desperately wanted a relationship with them; a child that was holding out hope for her parents' unconditional love.

When I started recovery work, my attempts at letting go deepened my loneliness and I often found myself on my knees, steeped in grief. Why? This was a question I asked God repeatedly. For a couple of years I hit a solid brick wall. Although I was learning and growing in many other areas, I simply could not let go of the hope of a real relationship with my parents; a loving, healthy adult relationship that would finally validate the child inside of me. I would often repeat the same cycle again and again and the old pains would resurface.

What would typically happen in these situations is that I would share too much personal information that they would later use against me or I would share on an emotional level that they did not understand. More often than not, if our conversations lasted more than a few minutes, their responses became extremely critical and sometimes just simply mean. As I learned more about alcoholism, I came to see how it can strip people of their compassion and sensitivity. In some cases even their humanity. In addition to the direct fallout from my parents' behavior, which of course was my hurt and disappointment, when the old pains resurfaced, my own character defects would flare up and my confidence in my own growth and healing would spiral downward.

Once I accepted I had to let go of my expectations for these primary relationships in my life, things became much easier. Already willing to change my own behavior, when I accepted I could not change theirs or the history we shared I was slowly released. I no longer expected my parents to be the understanding, concerned, engaged and loving parents I so desired and longed for. It simply was not going to happen.

My recovery work enabled me to distance myself emotionally so that I could periodically speak with them and see them for short periods of time without negative consequences. I learned to keep phone calls and visits both short and impersonal. I also learned to love them for who they were and where they were intellectually, emotionally, and spiritually. Despite all the pain they caused, there were parts of myself that I loved and respected and parts of my life that were positive and fulfilling. Even if they played no part in the person I wanted and continued to become, I tried to at least honor the role they did play in bringing me to this point in my life.

In addition to the relationship with my parents, one of the most heartbreaking relationships I had to let go of was the one with my older sister. As adults she was the only immediate family member with whom I shared any kind of bond. We shared a survivor bond as children and despite the tumultuous teens we stayed in touch throughout most of our young adult life. Unfortunately, we both lost touch with our brothers as they each struggled with their own challenges in overcoming our childhood experience.

After I left Brandon my sister and I rebuilt our relationship and made a conscientious effort to spend time together. When my niece and nephew were born I became a constant in their life. I regularly spent my vacations at their home and I would sometimes meet my sister and the kids at a mountain retreat. For a period of time there was some normalcy and my bond with my sister and her children filled my need for a family.

Because of our early childhood environment, my sister also grew up with a severely low sense of self-esteem and developed many of the other character traits of an adult child of an alcoholic. Unfortunately, she was not able to embrace recovery. Instead she married a man who is emotionally and physically abusive and she remains in that relationship today. In one situation after my brother-in-law put a gun to her head, I tried to walk her out the door. Despite the severity of the incident she stayed with him, bound by the childhood chains of fear and insecurity.

For many years I lived a codependent relationship with her. She was my big sister and I needed and wanted her in my life. Her compassion, kindness and sensitivity were qualities I loved and it broke my heart to see her stripped of these as she struggled to survive her abusive marriage. Her frantic phone calls were the worst. They came in at any time, at noon or two a.m. She was crying, on the edge, not knowing what else to do. She would tell me she was in the bathroom alone and I feared that this was the time it would all come to an end. I grieved heavily each time she called and I gradually and reluctantly learned when not to pick up the phone. I tried to convince her to leave her husband repeatedly, but my efforts were futile.

As I grew in awareness, I recognized the caretaker in me. My breaking point came when the abuse escalated and extended to my niece and nephew. As an aunt I researched my legal options and I discovered there were none. I sought counseling and learned that all I could do to prevent complete alienation from my sister and the children was take care of myself, try to stay in touch, and hope for the best. With my sister's refusal to file charges, and the children's inability to act on their own, there was nothing I could do. As the frequency and severity of the abuse cycle increased, there was a period of time I thought I might have a nervous breakdown. It was difficult for me to accept that my sister was allowing the cycle of family abuse to repeat itself; the anger and anxiety I experienced slowly drained the life out of me. In the end, to protect myself, I had no choice but to limit our relationship to the very minimum necessary to keep an open door for the children.

The one saving grace is the time I spent with my niece and nephew when they were younger. This created a bond that is still strong today and we continue to share a relationship despite the ongoing problems in their family. They have each come for an individual visit and we have discussed their feelings and fears with regard to their father and life at home. I'm confident that the time we've shared and my ability to be a witness to their experience will give them the strength and courage to reach out to me when they start having adult problems of their own.

With the help of the ACOA program I stopped judging my sister. Although she barely drank, the symptoms of the disease followed her into her own life and I learned through my ACOA experience that without help she may never be able to leave her abusive marriage. No amount of judgment is going to save her. Love, understanding, and healing are what she needs. I still remain open and hopeful that one day she will have the strength to take positive action for herself. When she does, I pray that I can be there to support her on her own journey to wholeness and self-love.

Friendship

While the relationships with my parents and sister were not the only unhealthy influences in my life, those relationships were my primary classroom for learning to set boundaries, take better care of myself, and learning my own personal limits. I eventually accepted I was not responsible for them and I could not change nor save them. As I gained confidence and learned how to manage the unhealthy relationships in my life, I was better able to identify and begin embracing the positive relationships. I gradually reconnected with Raphael and Louise and started making a more conscientious effort to stay in touch. I also started to actively pursue friendships that were good for me.

Early in my recovery I was very cautious about new friendships. The isolation I experienced as a child left me ill-equipped to build and maintain healthy boundaries. Trusting people was challenging. Although people showed genuine interest in befriending me, it was difficult to believe they would really like who I was if they knew the real me. Dismantling my barriers and simply letting people in was the first big step.

One of my greatest teachers in this area was my dear friend Anthony; another angel who came to my aid. The friendship was of significant importance, because he was my first male friend after I entered counseling. Although he was not involved in ACOA, he knew a little bit about my childhood as well as the challenges I faced learning to navigate life on my own. My relationship with Anthony grew out of our shared love of animals. In the warehouse where we worked together for three years, we frequently took in abandoned and stray cats until we could find them a home. We provided them a safe place to live and play in the back of the unused portion of the warehouse and we collaborated with our coworkers to purchase food and take care of any veterinarian needs. I often felt like a stray myself and this shared compassion for these animals created a bond between Anthony and me.

Anthony was an unusual man who wore his heart on his sleeve. To say he had skewed personal boundaries would be an understatement and sometimes his behavior concerned me. When I casually commented that Snickers was my favorite candy bar, I arrived at work the next day to find little brown wrappers spilling out of my refrigerator door. If I happened to hum a favorite new tune, the CD arrived in my CD player almost telepathically. It seemed Anthony was always paying attention to the little things. Anthony was also quick to offer his help and would innocently forget when I said I could do it myself. Many times I drove up to my house to find him sitting on my porch waiting for me.

Anthony's behavior frustrated me, but I was working my recovery program daily trying to remain open and grow beyond my previous limits. With my new tools, my frustration became a signal for me to stop and listen. What I heard from Anthony was I love you—No charge. I did eventually have to talk with him about respecting my personal boundaries, a definite moment of growth for me; but he took it graciously and remained my steadfast friend. Anthony was always there with a smile, an honest compliment, and a listening ear. He taught me that men can be trusted and counted on and he also showed me I didn't need to do everything on my own. When I reflect back on the friendship we've shared, I'm confident he was sent to teach me how to lean on people. Over the three years we worked together he became like an uncle to me and I slowly learned how to let people in.

Theresa was also a constant source of love, support and friendship in my life. She was a strong female role model for me and her years of experience with ACOA provided me a road map for healing and growth. She understood my struggles and experienced some of the same issues I did as an adult child of an alcoholic. She watched me vacillate between the highs and lows that come with recovery work and she loved me enough to let me fall apart. Each time I faltered she gently shined a light and helped me to see my true essence. She reflected back to me the love and strength in my heart and reminded me who I really am. I learned how to pick myself up and each time I was able to do it more quickly. With each personal achievement, she was there to champion and encourage me. She taught me that I was not my history and all the pain I carried from the past. She helped me see that I could choose differently.

As I grew and expanded my circle of friends there were many people who became dear to me. Each offered their own gifts and blessings that helped me become the person I wanted to be. With each success, my comfort zone expanded and I felt less and less alone. Today my friendships are a primary source of love and support in my life. I spend time nurturing the relationships from the past and I also pay attention to the new people who show up in my life. I no longer fear what people think. If I feel a connection I extend friendship and love openly, the way it has been extended to me.

Becoming Myself

The journey with other people of course brought me to the most important relationship of all—the relationship with myself. Prior to ACOA, I had no concept or understanding of what this was. As a child I was a shadow; a mere ghost of myself. The predominant rules in my family were don't talk, don't trust and don't feel. I became the person I needed to be to ensure my survival. I stayed out of the way, I did what I was told, and I thought and felt what they told me to think and feel. If I did not comply with my mother's wishes it would have resulted in total abandonment and complete emotional death. As I grew older, I recall many times when I tried to assert my own feelings, beliefs, or opinions. This of course was always met with criticism and condemnation. I recall being scoffed at or laughed at whenever I disagreed. "What, are you stupid?" is a rhetorical question I recall hearing often. Consequently I became a chameleon and as an adult I carried this behavior into every relationship whether it was with a friend, a professional connection, or an intimate partner. This of course left me feeling completely empty and hollow inside.

Releasing shame, developing a new belief system and working on my relationships was initially exhausting and discouraging. My experience was challenged by many false starts that kept me wondering if I was really capable of creating the change I needed to grow.

Each time I tried to reach down into the core of myself I had to wade through toxic pools of memories that were laced with shame, guilt, pain and misery. Each time I struggled to avoid the emotional undertow; many times I did not succeed. When I did get past the barriers, I realized I had no individual identity. There was simply no autonomous development during my childhood.

There were many times I wanted to give up and accept "good enough." If I had known in the beginning that the process could take years, I may have stopped before I got started. Luckily "One Day at a Time" was a slogan I learned early in recovery and it kept me on track when my soul got weary.

In ACOA I learned about enmeshment, the wounded inner child, and more about what happened to me. In a healthy, functional family it is the role of a parent to help a child develop an individual self with appropriate personal boundaries; a child that can learn to differentiate between her own needs and feelings and those of others. In a dysfunctional family, however, the child is seen as an object; a possession to validate the parent's ego and support the parent's unmet childhood needs. Because of this, the child never develops the skills to function independently or interdependently. The child becomes codependent, relying on the parents for her identity and survival. As a result, I became a list of negative character traits and survival tactics that had morphed together, rather than an individual unique human being. I did not know what I thought or truly felt about anything and I did not possess the ability to express my own personal being. What I heard when I did speak, in meetings or otherwise, was the voice of my mother and father and after a while it made me cringe. In order to survive and prevent myself from complete abandonment, I had become them.

Awareness and understanding were the first steps to healing and discovering my authentic self. As I became more aware of the disease and gained confidence through ACOA meetings, my new relationships, and my growing trust in God, I accepted that my parents suffered from a disease and that on some level they were not consciously aware of their own behavior. I began to realize that my parents carried their own toxic shame and started to see them as real people. They were simply faulty human beings who did not have the capacity to raise healthy functioning children, rather than the mean, unloving parents I perceived them to be. Each new bit of information about the disease and its negative effects armed me with the strength and courage I needed to continue to grow. It was very empowering for me to acknowledge the lonely child inside of me. In addition to building a relationship with my adult self, I also started nurturing and building a relationship with her. I knew it was now my job to take care of both of us. I had to consciously decide that I would face my history and stop the suffering. Suffering had become an addiction; a bad habit that was no longer serving me and I desperately wanted to become a happier more fulfilled person.

To recreate myself, I used the program to become more self-accepting and self-nurturing. I learned to forgive myself and I became much gentler with myself. I also began to create a loving home for myself in the present. I surrounded myself with people and things that inspired me and I created spaces at home that soothed and comforted me. As I became gentler with myself, I started to trust the new people in my life and I gave them a chance to get to know me and accept me. As these relationships developed, I started to feel loved and valued and my confidence grew. The old message "You are not lovable" started to fade into the background.

Through the love and support of the group, I learned that I could express my own feelings and needs and others would not abandon me. The group reflected back to me my positive qualities as well as my personal strengths, and this gave me the willingness and courage to continue to work on my weaknesses. I learned I was not the cause of, nor was I responsible for my parents or other people's feelings, thoughts, or behaviors and I slowly started paying attention to and taking care of my own. Eventually I was able to let down my guard and be more emotionally present and available without the constant fear of judgment or criticism.

I began to internalize my new feelings and behaviors and I was able to start replacing my old unhealthy belief system with a more nurturing, realistic one. With each new part of the foundation in place, I grew spiritually and emotionally and I learned how to manage my childhood prayer. Whenever life became intolerable or things seemed overwhelming, instead of reverting to isolation and hopelessness I relied on my new coping skills. I learned to reach inward and lean on my own personal strength as well reach out for the support of others. I began to not only trust but to truly feel that everything would be all right. Becoming more open and accepting of people ultimately led to a deeper understanding and acceptance of

God's love. I began to accept that I was not the unlovable worthless human being that I previously believed myself to be.

As I let go of my shame, my fears and irrational beliefs, and the unhealthy relationships in my life, I could see more clearly and I was no longer bogged down by the past. I then had the ability to explore my own emotional, intellectual and spiritual being. With this new discovery process I realized I was not the quiet, shy, compliant person that my parents raised to support their own image. Instead, as my confidence grew, I found I was quite the opposite and I embraced this person with a boldness I never knew I had.

I stayed in ACOA a lot longer than a month. While I was living in California, I attended group meetings for seven years and it was the most beautiful, healing time of my life. I achieved a sense of joy and happiness that I did not previously think possible. I became a core part of my ACOA group and I made many good friends who I consider part of my family today. My belief system has changed and I now know and truly believe that I am loved and worthy of a happy life. In addition, the knowledge, life skills, and relationships I developed through ACOA keep me from slipping into the abyss of self-pity and despondency that used to characterize my existence. I keep my angels near to my heart and practice daily gratitude for all they have given me. These days God and I are pretty tight. I lean into him easily now, knowing without a doubt that I am never alone. I am forever grateful for the program, the support of others, and the courage to look inward and become my true myself. I now stand on a firm foundation and my voice is truly my own. ACOA gave me a home and a family that taught me how to love myself and also how to let others' love in—two of the greatest gifts I have ever known.

Part III

A Final Gift

A Mother's Love

We are walking hand in hand along a crystalline white beach. The sun warms our backs as we kick sand along the shore. I look down at her soft blond hair and her big beautiful green eyes and her smile beams up at me. Her happiness elevates me; for a moment I feel as if I'm walking on air. She challenges me to a race and as we cross under the pier she jumps into my arms. "Twirl me," she says. It has become part of our routine. I grab her hands and we spin in circles until we are completely exhausted and fall to our knees in laughter. As I look into her eyes, I see she is me and I breathe a little more easily.

When the ghosts from the past periodically creep back into my mind, this is where I go to soothe myself. The child inside of me will always be there to remind me of the healing work I've done and the person I've become. I'd like to be able to say I am healed and I will never again have to live through the feelings of loneliness and despair that come from being an adult child of an alcoholic, but I know from experience that this is not true. Even as I wrote this manuscript, I struggled with lingering issues that poked at my consciousness. My healing continues and this too was part of the process.

It had been several years since I participated in active recovery work and on a cold November day in 2008, right before Thanksgiving, I received the phone call I had contemplated for a long time. My mother called to tell me she was dying. She had recently been diagnosed with breast and throat cancer and the prognosis wasn't good. At this point we did not have an active relationship. If we talked on birthdays and holidays that was a good year. Among the many medical details she shared that day, she also asked me to be the executor of her estate. She said she had not taken care of any of the paperwork and she hoped I would be willing to help out with the will as well as the funeral service. Her request was a painful reminder of the past. It was not the sons she loved so much or the favorite first daughter, but me, the one who wasn't good enough for either her or my father's unconditional love. For a brief moment I thought to decline her request, but the caretaker role prevailed and before I knew it I had agreed to everything.

I often wondered how I would feel when this time came and many people in my inner circle thought that I would or should be relieved. Oddly, it was quite the opposite. Knowing that my mother would soon be gone, my inner child started to panic. Although I had achieved a significant amount of growth and healing through ACOA and I had been caring for and nurturing my inner child for years, my mother's pending passing brought to my awareness one very indisputable fact; there is no substitute for a mother's love. Unknown to me, the little girl inside of me had still been holding onto hope until the very bitter end. I realized instantly that I would not only be grieving my mother's physical loss, but I would also be grieving the death of hope; the last hope that someday we would have a different relationship.

Wanting to receive closure on the years of pain, I started to fantasize about the conversation I would have with my mother before she passed away. I would tell her how she hurt me, how lonely I had been, and how I held onto the hope that we would one day share a loving mother/daughter bond. She would hug me, tell me she was sorry, and that she always loved me. Despite the past and all the pain I experienced, there was a small part of me that actually believed this was possible. As I prepared for my first trip to her Arizona home, I started crafting my script for this long overdue conversation.

In January I made the first of several trips to see my mother and to help her process the necessary paperwork and service arrangements. When I walked in the front door I was greeted by her companion Mark. I had not seen him in over 20 years, but even with age he looked the same to me. Mark was a longtime friend of my mother's, back when they were both married. After his wife passed away fifteen years earlier he and my mother reconnected. Although I did not understand the attraction, I was glad my mother was not alone and I was grateful for his support through what I knew would be a difficult process.

The throbbing in my chest started an hour earlier in anticipation of my arrival, but when my mother appeared at the end of the hallway my anxiety kicked up a notch. Disbelief and shock assailed me and snatched the very breath from my chest. If I had seen her on the street, I would not have recognized her. The alcoholism, the smoking, and ultimately the cancer had taken its toll. She was extremely thin and fragile and her ghostly appearance was made worse by her paper thin skin that looked as if it might fall off her bones.

After the hugs and hellos, and the other obligatory pleasantries, my mother needed to rest. When she took me into her bedroom where she now spent most of her time, once again, I couldn't believe my eyes. It was sad; a dirty and dismal room that looked more like a hospital room than someone's bedroom. There were medicine bottles and First Aid supplies stacked on the nightstand, dresser, and floor, and an IV drip hung on a medical cart next to the bed. The curtains and linens were a dull gray and dust moved across the floor as I lifted my feet. As we sat there talking and discussing what needed to be done, the mundane details that sum up a person's life, I felt the room closing in on me. It was not only the cancer, but a lifetime of sickness surrounding me. I had just arrived and I couldn't wait to leave.

Amazingly, despite her sickness, my mother still clung tightly to all of the negative energy, sarcasm, and meanness I lived with as a child. She had not changed a bit and because of the alcoholism her emotional intelligence was comparable to that of a 16 year old. She explained that she specifically asked me to take care of the will and funeral service because she knew my sister and brothers were not capable, nor smart enough. She said I was the smart kid and she was confident I would be able to take care of everything for Mark. It was the same kind of back handed compliment I received as a child and my heart ached for all of us. I thought how sad and lonely her life must have been, having four estranged children who wanted nothing to do with her.

Before that first day ended, I tossed my script in the trash. I knew without a doubt the conversation I prepared for was not going to happen. There would be no closure for the little girl inside of me and I would have to continue to take care of her on my own. I stayed for a week for that first visit and although I felt very sorry Mark I had mixed feelings and thoughts about my mother. There was a part of me that felt like she deserved it and sadly for a brief moment I was glad she was suffering. In that same moment, a wave of nausea rolled over me. These thoughts were not the thoughts of the person I worked so hard to become. Where was my compassion now? I wondered had I really grown past her influence and become a better person or was her meanness a part of me. On that day and throughout my visit, it seemed my own thoughts hurt me more than anything she could have ever done. My negativity weighed heavily on my mind and on the day of my departure, I couldn't get out of there fast enough.

In March, I went back for another visit. I had been receiving regular updates from Mark, and I knew this was the last time I would likely see my mother alive. On my drive down to Arizona, I was somber, not sure what to feel. Based upon my last visit, I knew that nothing about the relationship with my mother was going to change. I would have to continue to live my life never really knowing if she loved me. I contemplated what it would feel like when she was gone. Would I ultimately feel relief? Would I grieve? Would I finally be free of all the pain she had caused? I reflected on the disease and I mentally counted all the things it had stolen from me. I tried not to cry but the list grew long and the tears spilled down my cheeks.

When I arrived at her home, I gave myself a pep talk before I got out of the car. I thought about the healing I had accomplished and the person I worked so hard to become. I reminded myself of a book I recently read. It was Eckhart Tolle's *Power of Now* and it touched me deeply. Its message

"Be here now" promised a peace of mind if one could learn to transcend the ego and truly live in the present. I decided I would make the most of this last visit. There was no reason in these final days of my mother's life to recall the past or think about the future. I stayed four days the second time and at the end of my visit I felt relieved. I spent a significant amount of "now" time with my mother and I didn't dwell on what was or what might have been. We played Scrabble, watched *Jeopardy* and looked through old pictures. Amazingly, we even shared a little laughter. My behavior was aligned with the person I had become and I showed her the love, compassion, and forgiveness that I knew we both needed.

On Memorial Day weekend 2009 I received the final call from Mark. The doctors had given my mother a couple of weeks to live and it was time to make arrangements for her passing. Mark decided to admit her into a full time care facility since my last visit and I didn't blame him. Despite being in his eighties and suffering from ill health himself, he had cared for her until almost the very end. I felt comforted knowing that someone loved her. I notified family and friends and we met at the hospice center the following week. There were seventeen of us who gathered to say goodbye.

When we arrived at the hospice my mother was not lucid. She had been put in somewhat of a drug induced coma to help with the pain, and outside of the periodic guttural sound as if she was protesting against death, the first three days passed uneventfully. As we all circled around her bed we told stories, played music, sang, and tried to comfort each other the best we knew how. We read *Crossing Over*, a book provided by the hospice nurses that explains what happens to the body and the spirit in the final days and hours of a person's life. Every once in a while someone would break down in tears. I wondered what my sister and brothers were feeling as we grieved this final loss. I wondered about the eulogy I was asked to give. What do you say about someone that has caused you so much pain?

On June 15, 2009, the fourth day of our stay, the morning started much the same as the previous three. The lights were low and my mother's room was warm and very quiet. I was alone, slowly waking, listening to my mother's shallow breaths and the tick tock of the wall clock. The sound was somewhat meditative and I didn't notice when the nurses walked in the room. When I heard the door close, I looked up and noted the minute hand was approaching the nine. It was almost 6 am. On this particular morning, the nurses needed to give my mother a bath so I moved from what had become my permanent station at her bedside to a sofa chair in the far corner of the room. As I watched, I was amazed at how compassionate and conscientious they were. Not only were they caring for my mother with decency and respect, but they were also protecting me, shielding me from this harsh reality of life.

As I waited for them to finish, I reflected on the last nine months, from the time my mother was first diagnosed with cancer. In those months I processed a lifetime of loss and pain. I reflected on all the challenges I had to overcome to try and live a healthy, fulfilling life. I contemplated forgiveness. I believed I had forgiven her long ago, but I wondered now. Through the years I grieved for her, and for us, wondering where exactly her life took that fatal turn. As I sat there I found myself thinking, What if? Could it have possibly been different?

As the minute hand struck the twelve the nurse's voice shook me out of my daze. She said "Nyssa, I think she's ready to go." I got up, walked over to her bed, and gently cupped her feeble hands in mine. I was shaking a bit and I encouraged her to go. I talked about Cory and other family and friends, who she would now be able to see again. As the breath began to leave her, her pale wrinkled face turned alabaster smooth. A lifetime of pain drained from her body and for a brief moment she looked like a child; and then she was gone.

What happened next is still hard to believe. I do know, however, that much like my first experience with love, I felt it to my core. As my mother exhaled her last breath, my heart swelled, every hair stood on end, and goose bumps cascaded down my spine. A smile stretched from ear to ear and tears of joy rolled down my cheeks. With the veil and pain of the material world pushed aside, her spirit filled me and was able to express what I had been waiting for my entire life. For the first time in my life, I knew what it was. For the first time in my life, I felt my mother's love.

Ashes to Ashes

A month later at my mother's funeral service, I laid her ashes in the ground with my brother Cory. She wanted to be buried with him, so we transported her ashes back to his grave in San Diego. My initial concerns about writing and delivering the eulogy were unfounded and I discovered that my thoughts and words flowed easily. I told stories about some of her favorite family and friends and I talked about how happy she would be to see us all here, sending her off together. I also shared a few special words for Mark, expressing our gratitude as children for the love and companionship he brought to our mother's life and the support he provided us over the last couple of months as we all said goodbye.

After I delivered the eulogy, I sat there reflecting on my mother's life and her final days in the hospice. I remembered I could not leave her room. While everyone else went back to their hotels, I camped at her bedside each night. At the time

I could not explain why, but as I sat there at her grave I knew she had been keeping me there, knowing what I needed and possibly needing it more for herself. That final expression of her love freed us both from a lifetime of pain and sorrow and I was blessed to have been there to receive it. Love found a way and I am forever grateful.

Part IV

Recovery Tips

Introduction

Through my recovery experience, I've learned that healing and growing is an ongoing, lifetime process. I know the negative thoughts and behaviors associated with the survival roles I was forced to adopt can arise during times of stress and I often find there are areas where I can deepen my healing if I'm willing to do the work. Many times out of anger, frustration, or complete suffocating grief I have asked, "Why me." Why wasn't my childhood normal and happy? Why did I have to go through all this insanity? Why didn't they love me?

What I've learned by reading and associating with people who have shared a similar journey is that "Why me" is a completely useless and disempowering question. It keeps me in the victim role. The better more empowering question is, "What can I do now?" I would not wish my journey for anyone, but what happened to me is not as important as who I became. Despite it and in some cases because of it, I have lived and continue to live a healthy fulfilling life that is infused with more love than one person could expect in a lifetime. If I could have had a better childhood, parents who could express their love for me and nurture me in the way every child deserves, yes, of course, that would be ideal. But would I trade who I am, who I continue to become for the opportunity of a do over? Absolutely not; in many ways I believe I became who I am today because of what my parents, and more specifically my mother, couldn't give me.

Looking at my life from this perspective puts me in the survivor-hero role, which is much healthier and more productive. Although it took me many years to embrace this and quit asking why, I did eventually start living the concept. Today I know, regardless of what happened to me in the past, I am now responsible for my own growth and happiness, as well as my future. To help myself stay on track, I have identified key recovery steps that keep my emotions and behaviors in check and keep me moving forward despite any life challenges that may arise.

Tip #1 Seek Support

Asking for help can be challenging for even the most stable person with the most normal upbringing. For the adult child, however, asking for help can be extremely painful. In cases where emotional or spiritual support is being sought, where vulnerability is required, it can even be crippling. For me to take full advantage of my recovery work and to learn from the people who showed up in my life, I had to be willing to reach out; to extend beyond myself and trust that the support and encouragement I needed would be there for me.

Considering my shame based childhood this was no easy task. As evidenced by my desperate launch into counseling, I had to be on the very edge of life to ultimately accept that I needed help and actually have the courage to reach out. My fear and insecurity were a hindrance in counseling, ACOA meetings and my personal relationships. Often when I would talk about issues that were deeply personal, my voice would quake and I would look down at my hands. I was terrified of what people would think of me. I also did not have a lot of experience expressing my own thoughts and feelings. Counseling and the entire ACOA program were completely out of my comfort zone.

One of the concepts that I sincerely appreciated in ACOA meetings was the concept of no cross-talk. Cross-talk occurs when a group member interrupts as someone else is talking or later comments on what another member has shared. In ACOA meetings this is strictly prohibited and mentioned at the beginning of each meeting. When someone would mistakenly engage in cross-talk, the group peer pressure usually kicked in. Being able to talk in meetings without being interrupted, judged, or gossiped about was extremely healing for me. I believe this experience helped me find my voice and have the confidence to continue to seek support.

Unknown to me when I started ACOA I did have some practice in seeking support. When I reflect on the angels that showed up in my life, I recognize my willingness to change. Each time I was presented with an opportunity to take a different path, I stepped out and a bridge appeared. Being open and having the courage to grow was all I needed to do in some cases.

Loneliness is a common experience among adult children of alcoholics and the tendency to isolate a common behavior. For me these could be as addictive as alcohol to the alcoholic. I learned that when I felt most lonely and when I most wanted to isolate that those were the times that I really needed support from people who understood my experience. As I became more comfortable talking in meetings and started to make new ACOA friends, I pushed myself to reach out when I felt distressed. In the meeting I attended in California we shared a phone list that allowed the group members to network and stay connected. Spending time and talking with someone who could empathize was healing and comforting.

With my counseling, ACOA meetings and the love and support of good friends, I slowly learned it was okay to need help, ask for support, and embrace it when it showed up. Today when life's challenges arrive I no longer isolate. I reach for the nearest friend, attend a meeting, or if it's serious enough I may stop in to see my counselor. In contrast to what I learned growing up, I have come to understand that in life asking for support is not weakness, but strength instead.

Life is not meant to be lived alone.
* We cannot heal and grow on our own.*

Tip #2 Embrace Acceptance

One of the most challenging and painful lessons I had to learn was that I alone was responsible for healing my life. There was plenty of support, once I learned to reach out, but I was solely responsible for doing the necessary work. And I learned very quickly that recovery work is hard. It can be extremely painful, both emotionally and physically. Many times when some new insight would rise to the surface, the emotional pain buckled my knees and I would end up in the fetal position trying to comfort myself. This was definitely not an experience that encouraged continued introspection and growth.

For me this realization came with a lot of anger and resentment. The anger was boiling under the surface for a long time so when I started attending meetings and talking about what really happened, it came spewing forth like a volcano. I was angry at my parents. I was angry at God. I was angry at the Universe. I didn't understand why I had to clean up this mess, when it seemed I had nothing to do with creating it. I was very bitter when I learned just how much work was really ahead of me. Hadn't I already sacrificed enough? Didn't this disease already steal enough of my life? Because of this, I often experienced addictive cycles of anger and I would remain stuck in one recovery step for an excessive amount of time. I regularly and frequently regressed to the "Why me phase" and had myself a huge pity party. Often those parties lasted for weeks, even months, and I lost valuable, precious time in the process.

Eventually I realized I needed to move past this behavior and finally embrace the only solution. In order to move forward, I had to completely accept both the past and the present. I recognized I was a victim and I needed to honor the pain, but I did not need to continue to victimize myself. It was not my fault, but I was now responsible for healing and breaking the cycle. I had to acknowledge the facts. This is what happened. This is where I am now. Then I had to ask; What do I do now? Who do I want to become? What kind of life do I want to live?

Forgiveness, I was told by many well intentioned people, is the quickest route to acceptance, but forgiveness did not come easily for me. If I had waited on forgiveness, my recovery may likely have stalled indefinitely. Eventually, after trying to work the program for a short time, I recognized I did not necessarily need to forgive those whom I felt harmed me; at least not now. What I needed to do now was simply accept the circumstances. It didn't matter how I got to this point or who was at fault or if I forgave them. It only mattered where I was going from here. Two of my favorite slogans when I started attending meetings were "One Day at a Time" and "Let Go and Let God." Of course, leaning on God was nothing short of amazing for me, considering God almost kept me from starting the program.

Acceptance gave me a starting point for healing and once I accepted my circumstances I slowly learned to release them. Without acceptance, my denial and anger would have prevented any real, meaningful progress and forgiveness would have remained elusive.

Acceptance is the first step to forgiveness.

Tip #3 Practice Detachment

In addition to giving me a starting point for healing, acceptance also allowed me to detach from my emotional triggers in a healthy way. Detachment is not denial. I still validated and accepted my feelings and experiences, but I learned to manage them, rather than have them control me. Specific stressors for me included painful memories with my mother, negative behaviors, attitudes and influences of family members, and my own negative, present moment feelings and behaviors that needed to be changed. I knew that I needed to spend time exploring my personal story in order to grow and move past my history, but it was extremely difficult to avoid becoming entrenched in negativity when I was processing years of confusion, resentment, anger, sadness, and fear. In order to keep moving forward, I had to learn to detach both physically and emotionally.

Physical detachment for me involved limiting contact with family members and other people that I knew had a toxic effect on my emotional well-being. These were people I knew who were stuck in the dysfunction and extensive association with them did not serve my healing. Initially this created an even deeper loneliness in me, but as I began to heal I recognized the value. The more I limited my association, the better I felt. The better I felt, the more I was able to limit my contact without feeling so lonely. I eventually learned to recognize people who were healthy or at least on a healing path and instead of reaching back into my past when I needed a friend or a listening ear, I began reaching forward into my future.

Emotional detachment required a bit more mental gymnastics. In addition to distancing myself from people, I also had to detach from painful memories and my own current circumstances. Although it was difficult for me to accept, when I started exploring my history and working through the recovery concepts, I recognized how dysfunctional many of my thought processes and behaviors were. The upside for me was that it seemed that most of my thoughts and behaviors hurt only me, not others. This gave me some relief, but I came to realize the negative patterns prevented me from reaching my full potential and becoming the person I was intended to be. In addition, if left unaddressed I knew I would continue the cycle of negative behavior and would likely never be fully happy.

I managed my emotional detachment with good self-care and present moment awareness. One of the most valuable messages that I heard in recovery was "Be gentle with yourself." Many of the readings we discussed in ACOA meetings talked about becoming your own loving parent; taking care of yourself the way any healthy parent would care for a child. A healthy parent makes corrections out of love to enable the child to grow and function as a contributing member of society, not to shame or blame them. Whenever I would start berating myself about a negative behavior or thought pattern, I would stop and repeat, "Be gentle with yourself, be gentle with yourself." I would do this as long as it took for the moment to pass. In addition, I would visually stop the old negative tapes in my head and remind myself to focus on the now. When I focused on the now I could let go of the person in the old tapes and redirect the current thoughts and behaviors to be more aligned with my future self.

For painful memories I used a visualization exercise where I placed these memories in a room and locked the door. I then would only unlock this door for the specific purpose of healing and I would only do it when I was in a safe place with supportive friends. As I progressed in my recovery I dealt with most of these memories, one by one, and I grieved for the lonely, hurt child inside of me.

The grieving process is a very important part of the healing process. Until I grieved my loss, I could not fully let go of the past. Ultimately, detachment allowed me to create a distance from the negative influences in my life. The distance then allowed for healing and growth. Although it took consistent sustained effort, I was no longer overwhelmed by the enormity of the problems and I was able to stay focused in the present moment, which was the only place I could begin to heal.

Detachment creates a space where healing can begin.

In the Heart of a Child

Tip #4 Allow Forgiveness

Forgiveness is an age old healer and one of the earliest natural remedies for just about every physical, emotional, and spiritual affliction known to humankind. There is not a book, magazine, or article that addresses healing and personal growth that does not mention forgiveness in some regard. Although I believe forgiveness is important and necessary, I struggled with it when I viewed it as an action that I had to take. As mentioned earlier, I dealt with a lot of anger when it came to accepting I was responsible for healing my life. As a survivor, I was often insulted when people would tell me I needed to forgive. If only they knew how callous their words sounded. I felt I had enough work to do, so having responsibility for something as ominous as forgiveness for my offenders was just too overwhelming for me.

Through recovery I developed an idea that worked much better for me and instead of focusing on forgiveness as an active process, I learned to allow forgiveness as part of the natural healing process. Allowing forgiveness was much more manageable for me. The way I allowed forgiveness was by doing my own healing work and by not resisting forgiveness when it did show up. I learned to discipline the toddler. Instead of stomping my feet and crossing my arms in resistance and indignation, I was open and embraced forgiveness when it arrived. I started recognizing an interesting pattern. Forgiveness often arrived on the heels of compassion and more specifically on the heels of self-compassion. Often, as an adult shame-based child, I was brutal with myself. I followed in my mother's footsteps. I could do nothing right. In ACOA meetings, I would often refer to myself as a jerk. Although the hurt was caused by indirect behaviors such as withholding, dishonesty, or irresponsibility, the impact on others was still negative.

As I grieved my losses, grew in self-awareness, and became my own loving parent, I developed self-compassion and learned to forgive myself. With this, I became much more tolerant and accepting of my own faults and mistakes and I was then more easily able to extend this understanding to others. I also began to understand the pain that causes people to engage in destructive behavior patterns and I became willing to let myself and others off the hook. This became a healing cycle that I recognized and welcomed.

When I began recovery work, I did not yet understand that forgiveness was a gift for me, but I eventually learned that in order to fully heal I needed to heal my resentments. I needed to forgive those who had harmed me, including myself, and understand that the behaviors were the result of sickness. It took me many years, but before my mother passed away I did forgive her. I also grieved for her and her life. I often wondered what fateful turn the road took to bring her such pain and addiction. When I forgave her, when I dismantled that final barrier that protected me for so long, I could finally breathe. My heart was now fully open and I could more easily let love in.

When I am struggling with resentments and forgiveness today, I look for the lessons and try to remain open. I remind myself that when I am withholding forgiveness from someone else, I am withholding it from myself.

Learn self-compassion and forgiveness will follow.

Tip #5 Break the Cycle of Avoidance

Learning to actively process negative feelings and emotional pain and coming to understand it is a normal, necessary life skill was a revelation for me when I started recovery work. Because I watched my parents stuff their own feelings and pain with alcohol, I didn't learn how to manage mine. There was no one to teach me and of course the hurts continued to pile up for the first twenty-eight years of my life. When the pain became intolerable, I would ignore it and bury it with alcohol, stimulants, food, shopping, exercise or any other behavior that would offer escape.

My favorites were exercise and shopping. The amount of time and money I wasted with these distractions is almost comical. There were times I exercised to the point of physical pain and shopped until I was completely broke. I can laugh about it today, but it took me a very long time to recognize what I was doing. Although engaging in these activities is perfectly fine if done in moderation, any activity that is used to avoid dealing with feelings is unhealthy. As I began to focus on and take care of my emotional body, the addictive behaviors started to fall away. Although there are times I may still delay in appropriately addressing issues, recovery work has mostly freed me from the cycle of avoidance. Today I am keenly aware when I am headed down a negative or destructive path and I can actively use my skills to redirect myself. The three steps I use today to ensure I fully process my feelings and any subsequent emotional pain are acknowledgment, discovery, and release.

Acknowledgment is the first and most important step for me. Like many people, I feel stress in a particular part of my body. I have learned that discomfort in my shoulders and spine is a good indicator that emotional distress is pending or there is some unresolved issue. If I already know what's causing the stress (i.e. I'm feeling violated, because I've just been lied to) acknowledgment is relatively easy. I will usually verbalize it for myself so I can hear the facts (i.e. Karen just lied to my face. I am so pissed!). Once I do this, I can move on to releasing it. If the physical symptoms present themselves and I am not aware of the cause, which is the case when my emotional reaction to an event is delayed, then the acknowledgment is a little more difficult. In this situation, I will have to move on to the second step, which is discovery, so that I can determine the exact nature of the stressor.

Discovery involves a recounting of recent events and possible triggers for my emotional response. In this situation I usually talk to myself. I have found talking out loud helps bring the story out more quickly. I'll start by telling myself what I'm feeling. For instance, I'll say I feel sad, I feel anxious, I feel angry, I feel violated. Whatever the feeling is, I give it life with words. Making it real is very important to me. As a child my feelings were either shamed or denied, so honesty and openness with myself is critical. After I name the feeling, I start exploring recent events both at work and home. Was there a particular exchange I had with someone that upset me? Did someone hurt my feelings? Did I do something I feel guilty about? Is the date or period of time of significance (i.e. holidays, Mother's Day, etc.)? Once I identify the event, I talk through it with myself. This helps me process the event and determine if there is any action I need to take. I have found that I need to put a stop gap (a definitive period of time) on this part of the process, because sometimes I become addicted to reliving the story. There are times I have rehashed a story thousands of times in my mind before moving on. This is not healthy and is counterproductive. Once I talk through the story, and identify the stressor, I determine if there is any action I need to take. If there is something I can do, then I know I need to take that action first before I can release and let go of the stressor. If there is nothing I can do about the situation, I've learned to quickly move on to the third step of the process.

Release is the final step and can sometimes be the most difficult. It's easy to become addicted to the pain and take on the martyr role. When it involved other people holding onto my anger, resentments, and disappointments allowed me to maintain a protective barrier of superiority. When the issue was directly related to my own behavior, it was difficult because I still struggled with many irrational beliefs. Some of these included the need to be perfect, the need to be approved by all the significant people in my life, and feeling responsible for everyone and everything. There were times I would make a mistake and relive the experience for days and sometimes even weeks.

For me, release is taking action to make positive change and let go of the pain and guilt. I learned to free others to be themselves and allowed others to make their own mistakes and be responsible for their own behavior. I also began taking responsibility for myself and I learned to let myself off the hook. I did not need to be perfect. If I was struggling with the letting go I would use techniques I learned in ACOA. Writing letters was very healing for me. In cases where there was nothing I could do about the stressor; the act of writing gave me an outlet. I actually felt like I was taking action and it empowered me and gave me the strength to move forward. Visualization of the release was also helpful. When I used this technique, I most often put my pain in a box and then hiked to my favorite lookout. At the peak I would open the lid and dump the contents over the edge. As I visualized all my pain and hurt being carried away with the wind, I felt release and renewed hope.

My own present moment well-being became more important than anything that happened in the past, even if it was just yesterday. After several years in recovery, I recognized how much lighter I felt. I was no longer carrying all the stuffed feelings from the past and I was not allowing myself to ignore new issues that would arise. I truly became an active participant in my own healing and began creating the emotional life that I wanted. I started experiencing not only happiness, but real, profound and sustained joy.

Embrace and process negative emotions and feelings.

Tip #6 Recognize and Change Negative Behavior Patterns

As I became better at seeking support and more comfortable processing my negative feelings and emotions, I started to focus on more specific behaviors that I knew were no longer serving me. One of my biggest challenges was my perfectionism. I was brutal with myself and consequently every step forward involved two, three, or four steps backward. Because I was never enough for my mother, I grew up not being able to recognize or accept my own qualities and successes. I spent an excessive amount of time obsessing and trying to perfect every aspect of my life which included my relationships, my job, my appearance, etc. I basically became my mother and continued to victimize myself.

My behavior created a level of diligence that exhausted me and consequently I was never able to be fully present. When I was younger, I was not entirely conscious of this pattern and others did not necessarily see my behavior as something negative. Many people, including myself, just thought I was an overachiever. Of course my perfectionism served me well with my academics and professional pursuits, but in the long run it was at too great a cost. Through recovery work, I learned my personal standards were unreachable and that my pursuit of such high standards detracted from my personal satisfaction and happiness.

Learning to silence my inner critic was the first step in overcoming my perfectionism. The critic was initially my mother's voice, but as I got older it became my own. It ran on the old, automated tapes in my head and I did not have to take any action to give it the stage. In ACOA, I learned that I had the power to stop it. I learned that I could replace it with a gentler, more positive voice that was encouraging and supportive. When I started doing this I became much more accepting and understanding of my personal limitations. Learning to let go of results was also helpful in overcoming perfectionism. As an adult, part of the drive for me to be perfect was about control. It gave me a sense of being in control of myself as well as my environment. Learning to do my best and release the rest to the universe was very healing for me. It took time, but with practice the intensity of my hypervigilant behavior eventually began to lessen.

Setting limits became an effective tool. If I was working on a specific project, I decided at the start on a certain timeframe for completion and on a specific number of reworks. Once I reached that pre-determined limit, I forced myself to let go and move to the next step. In some cases I had to talk myself through it. Other times, I would make a commitment to someone else knowing it would interrupt my flow and help propel me forward.

My perfectionism also played a role in my distorted body image. Although my mother's treatment of me and the sexual abuse were both factors, I continued to victimize myself as an adult by trying to have perfect looks. I had to have perfect hair, a perfect face, and a perfect body. As I worked on my inner critic I became much easier on myself, but it wasn't enough to transform my body image. Early in my recovery, I was introduced to a mirror technique that was very helpful for me. I would stand or sit in front of a full length mirror completely undressed. I started with my eyes and as I looked into my eyes I told myself "I love you." I then moved to each area of my body and repeated the process. I always finished back at my eyes. I was very shy about this technique when I first tried it, but after trying it a few times I fully embraced its power. The love I learned to show myself was nurturing and healing. I grew to sincerely love myself, with all my humanness and perceived faults. My loving mirror reflected back to me who I really was and I experienced a love I had never known. I've done a significant amount of body image work over the years, but I still periodically obsess about my looks and my appearance. These days when I find myself being obsessive about my body, I don't necessarily need my mirror. I can simply acknowledge the thoughts and talk to myself. This allows me to verbalize and honor my feelings and I'm usually able to move past it quickly. If I ever feel the need, I know my loving mirror is there for me.

In addition to being a perfectionist, I also had an over developed sense of responsibility. In my family, I took on the caretaker role to keep the peace and to ensure my security. I often felt guilty if I took care of my own needs. Because of this I did not develop a good sense of self and as an adult I became a people pleaser. Caring for and focusing on my own needs was something I had to learn and practice with my new ACOA family. With practice, I learned to ensure my needs were being met before I tried to support others.

Learning to say no was a major step for me. I also quit minimizing my needs, as if they were not as important as others. This practice was very difficult for me, especially in romantic relationships. I feared sharing my real feelings because I thought the person would no longer want to be with me. I ultimately learned that a healthy relationship, romantic or otherwise, involves two people who care equally about their own as well as the other person's feelings and needs.

Overcoming my perfectionism and learning to manage my over-responsibility were key steps in helping me take better care of myself. The more I learned to care for myself, the more I was able to embrace my own individuality. It was during this time I started writing. I used a journal to document my thoughts and feelings and I started making observations about what made me happy and what inspired me. I started thinking a lot about who I wanted to be. There were people in my group meetings that I admired and I would note their behaviors and try to incorporate those into my life. As I worked through my negative behavior patterns, I began creating new ones that were more nurturing and supportive. I ultimately came to see this process of re-creation as the pinnacle of self-care. I did not have to default to the adult of my childhood experience. I could choose who I wanted to become.

*Create behavior patterns that support
the person you want to become.*

Tip #7 Affirm Your Highest Self

Monitoring and managing my internal and verbal dialogue was critical in achieving growth through my recovery work. Thoughts and words have the power to transform. I, like many adult children, had been conditioned by my caregivers to denigrate and demean myself, rather than think and speak in a way that builds a positive self-image. Because of this I fed my mind a daily dose of toxic sludge, which created barriers to my personal growth and happiness. My awareness was critical in changing this behavior. Through recovery I learned about the power of positive thinking and the use of affirmations to change my own negative thoughts. Use of a daily, positive affirmation helped me plant seeds that ultimately helped me grow beyond my self-imposed limitations.

Affirmations most often start with an "I" statement (I am, I respond, I choose, I accept, etc.) and are deeply personal. I learned it was best not to share my affirmation with anyone who did not fully support and understand my efforts. Initially I had one affirmation, but as I continued to grow I developed many and each evolved as I began to change. I used a brainstorm approach in developing my personal affirmations and I wrote down qualities and characteristics that described my ideal self and my ideal life. I thought about the people in my new ACOA family and I jotted down character traits that resonated with me or that I found valuable.

I used multiple affirmations throughout my early recovery and I still use one today to nurture my highest self and achieve success and happiness in my life. My current personal affirmation developed out of a series of "I am" statements that turned into a short narrative. It starts like this: "I am healthy, I am happy, I am loved. I am a great listener and I share a bond with people." Once I created my affirmation I wrote it down and now I think, read and speak it daily. Speaking it out loud is very important in maximizing the transformative power of my thoughts and words. I need to hear over and over again the person I want to continue to become. I know I need to believe I am already that person.

When affirming positive change in my life, I quickly became aware that what usually comes first is a great degree of challenge. It often came from several different directions and affected many different aspects of my life. I would often feel discouraged and be tempted to give up. I learned, however, that this is the time my fortitude is most needed. There is no way to get from where I am now to where I want to be and from who I am now to who I want to become without growth and change. When the rough seas roll in I hold on tight and affirm even more frequently and more loudly. The storms, I now know, will eventually pass.

Using affirmations has helped me become more aligned with my authentic self. In addition to now being able to create my world with my thoughts and words, I believe my healing work has allowed me to peel back the layers of my spiritual being and tap the soul that was never allowed to truly develop. I sincerely believe who I continue to become was already a part of who I was supposed to be. It has just taken me a lot longer to show up, because of the lack of loving parents to nurture me.

Use your thoughts and words to affirm your highest self.

Tip #8 Nurture the Relationship with Yourself

Discovering my authentic self has been one of the greatest experiences of my life. Exploring my own emotional, spiritual and intellectual being, discovering my passions and innate talents, and deciding exactly who I want to be has been very empowering and a significant part of my recovery process. When I started recovery I had no concept of a relationship with myself, but today I know that this is one of the most important relationships I will ever have. It is also the foundation for every other relationship I will ever experience. To ensure my foundation maintains its integrity, I continue to practice self-compassion and self-care and I continue exploring and nurturing the relationship with myself.

Self-compassion and self-care evolved through my recovery years. In the beginning it simply meant attending meetings, spending time with my new ACOA friends, and reading books that taught me about the disease and its impact on children. Eventually I expanded my focus to ensure I was addressing all aspects of my life. This included my physical, emotional, and spiritual well-being. Fitness became very important to me. This was not the excessive activity I previously engaged in to keep my body perfect, but rather a more balanced behavior that I used to ensure I stayed physically and emotionally healthy. Exercise became a way for me to clear out the mental clutter and release any lingering stress. It limited the amount of stress in my life then freed me up to focus my energy elsewhere. I also became more aware of what I was eating and I tried to avoid sugars and highly processed foods that I knew would negatively impact my emotional body.

Developing new friendships, engaging in new activities, and ensuring I did not spend too much time alone was also very important for me. It was very easy for my inner critic to engage the old tapes if I had idle time on my hands. I tried not to overextend myself, but at the same time I ensured I had regularly scheduled activities that gave me something to look forward to. In addition, I explored my new relationship with God and came to a point of understanding that I didn't need to have all the answers. I could choose the God of my understanding and take it a day at a time. With this, I quit looking for love in relationships and learned to love myself and focus on God's love instead.

Part of nurturing the relationship with myself involved spending scheduled time alone. I found that a weekly allotment of private time is what worked best for me. If I didn't get enough time alone it was almost guaranteed that not only would my mood and attitude quickly deteriorate, but also my physical well-being. During my private time I would meditate, journal, walk, talk to myself or do any number of things that nurtured my soul.

Meditating is very calming for me. It helps me relax my body and quiet my mind. It is a practice that allows me to check in with myself. When I am meditating, I am more likely to notice if there is anything I need to address that may be upsetting me or if there's something I need to let go. The first time I experienced deep meditation I awakened and cried for two hours. There was so much unresolved pain below the surface. It took me a month to reengage my courage to try again, but today it is a regular part of my routine. Journaling and talking to myself help me process my thoughts and feelings. The physical act of writing is always comforting and healing and it helps me keep track of my continued progress in each area of my life. Talking to myself sometimes helps me bring issues to the surface, and I often use it as a brainstorming technique for problem solving. There are also times that I simply talk to myself for the company.

Through the years I've learned that spending time in nature and working with animals are the two activities that nurture me the most. When I am hiking out under a big blue sky or cuddling with the cats and kittens at the adoption center, I feel a timeless awareness and I exist in a state of joy that cannot be defined. Ensuring I fit these activities into my schedule gives me focus and perspective and infuses me with energy, hope, and love. I can then better take care of my inner child, my adult self, and those others who are part of my journey.

Schedule time to nurture the relationship with yourself.

Tip #9 Associate with Positive People

A critical component of my recovery was managing my time. This included what I was doing, as well as who I was doing it with. Spending time with the right people, as well as avoiding people who I knew were not good for me was a practice I had to learn. Because of the ingrained negative self-talk and codependent behaviors that were a result of association with my biological family, I often attracted people who had similar negative character traits. Unfortunately, many of these people were willing to feed my negativity. They were the blamers and complainers, stuck in the problem with no interest in solutions. They could suck the positive energy out of a room and put a negative spin on even the most inspiring story. They were not interested in growth or change and I learned the only healthy approach was to avoid them. It took me a long time to be able to identify these people, so I often invested a considerable amount of time in a relationship before seeing the red flags.

Once I started recovery work, mentoring and positive association were critical for my personal growth. To ensure I didn't get stuck and repeat my old negative patterns it was extremely important for me to spend time with healthy, positive, forward thinking people. These people were often on their own healing, seeking journey. They lifted me up and reflected back to me my true essence; they helped me work through the rough patches and congratulated me when I made it through another phase of my healing; they encouraged me to become my best self; they let me fall apart, so I could learn how to pick up the pieces in a healthy way and they loved me even when I couldn't. They created a safe space for the necessary reflection and feedback to help me grow beyond my history into the person I was intended to become. They became my own loving family.

One of the most beautiful experiences I've ever had involved an intimate sharing at one of my birthday celebrations. As part of our dinner finale we participated in a birthday tradition that my friends started with their foster children years ago. We started with the birthday girl, and each person around the table shared what they most valued about me. After my turn was complete we did this for each of the other three people who were at dinner that night. As I was sitting there receiving, absorbing all of the expressions of love and gratitude, my eyes filled with tears. It was difficult for me to take it all in. It was equally emotional when I was sharing my own thoughts with each of my friends. As I was reminded of how amazing they each were I felt a deep gratitude, thankful that they were a part of my life here with me now. Later I wondered what would happen if every child and adult were treated to this experience throughout their lifetime. What if all families loved each other with such openness and vulnerability? What a tremendous gift and validation for the soul.

I have learned that family extends much farther than my biological ties. In many cases real family has no biological ties. I heard someone say it nicely; a family is a community we choose and includes the people we choose to love and those who choose to love us. Today I continue to reach out and expand my circle of positive, healthy, forward thinking people. I can easily spot like-minded people and I quickly identify people who are not healthy for me. When I meet someone my spirit resonates with, someone I feel good with,

I extend love and consciously take the time to nurture the relationship. I am now able to seek true intimacy with both myself and others.

Create your own loving family.

Tip #10 Extend Beyond Yourself – Make It Matter

I have found that giving back completes the circle of healing. In addition to helping me become my best self, it also helps me to continue to nurture the child inside of me. I know based upon my recovery work that this child will likely be with me for the rest of my life and it is my responsibility to nurture her and love her. Part of this process is ensuring she knows she does not walk alone and the best way to do this is to help other people.

I now believe my purpose in life, and one of the keys to reaching my highest potential, is to identify my talents and use them to serve others. As I progressed through recovery, it became very important for me to make my life matter. "Make it matter" became one of my regular mantras. Part of this was simply because of all the pain I experienced. I thought it would be a waste to have survived my experience and not put it to some good use. I also came to deeply believe I did not survive and find ACOA by pure chance. I came to believe I showed up for a reason.

I started to pursue my higher purpose by supporting my fellow ACOA members on their own journey and also by supporting organizations I believed in. I did this by volunteering and by donating money. In the beginning I approached this in a very unhealthy way. As I was still learning to love myself, deep down I was acting on a belief that if I could do enough, give enough, matter enough that I would be lovable.

I often gave an excess of time and money that I did not have and this made me exhausted and resentful. Through ACOA I learned that I was already lovable and I already mattered just for having shown up in my life. There was no amount of giving, doing, or achieving that was ever going to fill the hole in my soul that existed from not having a loving bond with my parents.

Once I got past this, I moved from a **doing** existence to a **being** existence and I was more able to find satisfaction and fulfillment spending time with people and pursuing my passions. In discovering my passions I learned to focus on what made me lose track of time and when I felt most alive. I learned to trust the signals my body was sending me and I paid attention when I felt not only happiness, but real sustained joy. I increased my self-awareness by exploring new social environments, hobbies, and cultural events that expanded my world view. In addition to spending time with Mother Nature and volunteering with animals, I've learned that I also enjoy speaking, teaching, and working with at-risk adults and youth. Today I try to focus my time and resources in these areas, always reminding myself to maintain a healthy balance of giving and receiving. I have learned that real joy comes not only from living in my purpose, but allowing others the opportunity to live in theirs as well. As I continue on my journey of healing and self-discovery, I hope that I can inspire others to extend beyond themselves and use their own experiences to make a positive change in the world.

Cultivate your passions and talents.
Be of service and live in joy.

A Message of Loving Support

On a particularly difficult day, one of those days you hope someone is thinking about you and praying for you, I received a note from my dear friend Theresa. Theresa was not only a friend, but she was my ACOA mentor and I considered her a big sister. She was one of my angels and as I read her words, her love filled my heart. In a few simple sentences she validated me and all the hard work she knew it took to overcome my childhood and become my authentic self. I keep this letter nearby, so when the road gets long I can draw on her strength. If you relate to my story, I now extend this support to you. I wish you the comfort of angels as you embrace your own journey of healing and self-discovery.

Dear Nyssa
I'm so glad our paths crossed and we get to walk together on the mountain trail of life. In case I haven't told you face to face lately, I want you to know how much I admire you. I admire your courage and willingness to take a look at those things that are difficult to look at. It has been a blessing to witness you coming out the other side of a difficult upbringing—a Victor!
You are a powerful lady and a powerful teacher!
With love always!
Theresa

Part V

Resources

Books

I believe reading is the foundation of personal growth and healing. Personal growth enables me to nurture my best self and achieve my highest potential. Coming from a family entrenched in alcoholism, I found it very important to educate myself on the disease and grow beyond the limitations set for me by my family of origin. For a couple of years I read everything I could get my hands on. My understanding of what happened to me and why I felt and behaved as I did was critical for me to begin healing. I highly recommend daily reading as part of any recovery program. It can be a book, magazine article, blog etc., as long as it is educational, positive, and encourages healing and personal growth. Following is a list of some of my favorite ACOA books that I regularly read for inspiration and understanding. I have also included another list of educational and inspirational books and resources that came to me through my ACOA recovery program. I am forever grateful to the authors who invested the care and time to share their messages.

ACOA Book List

- *The Twelve Steps for Adult Children*—Anonymous
- *Thou Shall Not Be Aware*—Alice Miller
- *The Drama off The Gifted Child*—Alice Miller
- *Healing The Shame That Binds You*—John Bradshaw
- *Bradshaw On The Family*—John Bradshaw
- *Family Secrets*—John Bradshaw
- *Homecoming*—John Bradshaw
- *The Language of Letting Go*—Melody Beattie
- *Codependent No More*—Melody Beattie
- *Beyond Codependency*—Melody Beattie
- *Each Day A New Beginning*—Karen Casey
- *Change Your Mind and Your Life Will Follow*—Karen Casey
- *The Little Book of Letting Go*—Hugh Prather
- *Adult Children of Alcoholics*—Janet G. Woititz, Ed.D
- *The Struggle for Intimacy*—Janet G. Woititz, Ed.D
- *Healthy Parenting*—Janet G. Woititz, Ed.D

Other Helpful Books

- *How to Stop Worrying and Start Living*—Dale Carnegie

- *The Way of the Wizard*: Twenty Spiritual Lessons for Creating the Life You Want—Deepak Chopra

- *Change Your Mind, Change Your Life*—Gerald G. Jampolsky, M.D., and Diane V. Cirincione

- *Love is the Answer: Creating Positive Relationships*—Gerald G. Jampolsky, M.D., and Diane V. Cirincione

- *Love is Letting Go of Fear*—Gerald G. Jampolsky, M.D.

- *Goodbye to Guilt, Releasing Fear Through Forgiveness*—Gerald G. Jampolsky, M.D.

- *The Seven Spiritual Laws of Success*—Deepak Chopra

- *The Choice*—Og Mandino

- *The Greatest Miracle in the World*—Og Mandino

- *The Return of the Ragpicker*—Og Mandino

- *The Road Less Traveled*—M. Scott Peck, M.D.

- *The People of the Lie: The Hope for Healing Human Evil*—M. Scott Peck, M.D.

- *A Return to Love*—Marianne Williamson

- *A Course in Miracles*—The Foundation for Inner Peace

Fellowships and Organizations

Adult Children of Alcoholics	http://adultchildren.org/
Alcoholics Anonymous	http://www.aa.org/
Al-Anon and Al-Ateen	http://www.al-anon.alateen.org/
The Chopra Center	http://www.chopra.com/
Foundation for Inner Peace	http://acim.org/
Jampolsky Outreach Foundation	http://jerryjampolsky.com/
The Center for Attitudinal Healing	http://www.healingcenter.org/
The Awareness Center	http://www.drjan.com/
Hazelden, A Part of the Hazelden Betty Ford Foundation	http://www.hazelden.org/

www.ingramcontent.com/pod-product-compliance
Lightning Source LLC
Chambersburg PA
CBHW020546030426
42337CB00013B/981